economists know about productivity with the findings of organizational theorists about worker motivation, he describes a strategy to improve what has come to be called the "quality of worklife," with major benefits for both employers and employees.

After discussing the history of the current inflation/unemployment dilemma, Stern explains how certain improvements in quality of worklife will tend to make full employment more sustainable and how keeping unemployment rates down in the short run will encourage employers, unions, and employees to make such improvements. He presents several ways in which state, local, and federal governments can promote quality of worklife, productivity, and full employment. In the final chapter, he describes how some profitmaking enterprises have already adopted parts of the proposed strategy, and how the payoff is likely to increase as more companies put the strategy into practice.

About the Author

A specialist in the economics of human resources, **David Stern** earned a Ph.D. in Economics and City Planning at the Massachusetts Institute of Technology. He taught economics at Yale University and is now Associate Professor of Education at the University of California, Berkeley.

MANAGING HUMAN RESOURCES

MANAGING HUMAN RESOURCES

The Art of Full Employment

DAVID STERN
University of California, Berkeley

Auburn House Publishing Company
Boston, Massachusetts

Permission is gratefully acknowledged for reproduction of the statement by
Irving Bluestone from *Viewpoint*, the quarterly magazine of the Industrial
Union Department, AFL-CIO; and the material in Tables 3.1 and 3.2,
originally published by the Institute for Social Research, University of
Michigan.

Library of Congress Cataloging in Publication Data
Stern, David S., 1945–
   Managing human resources.

   Bibliography: p.
   Includes index.
   1. Job enrichment. 2. Work environment. 3. Personnel
management. I. Title.
HF5549.5.J616S74   658.3'142   81-20517
ISBN 0-86569-097-9   AACR2

Printed in the United States of America

For J. and R.

FOREWORD

Economics is full of dandy paradoxes, troubling conundrums, apparent contradictions, and counterintuitive notions. For example, economists say that when the income of workers is significantly increased, they either will work more or they will work less. A moment's thought shows this academic double-talk to be true: some people will take their higher income and run (using it to support increased time for vacations, schooling, leisure or family activities); others will be motivated to work more when they earn more. While true, this is hardly *useful* information.

But understanding the even tougher economic paradox addressed in this book can provide useful guidelines for policy makers. Here are the phenomena David Stern analyzes: (1) Evidence indicates that workers who have secure jobs tend to be less productive than those who do not have job security; (2) evidence also indicates that workers are willing to cooperate with management to improve productivity only when their jobs are secure. Let's run that by again: (1) Workers with tenure do not work as hard as those without tenure. That much squares with our observations of teachers and civil servants. But (2) is a harder concept to swallow: that workers need job security before they will make efforts to improve their productivity doesn't appear to square with what we know about (1).

But both pieces of evidence are factual (and compatible with each other), as Stern goes on to demonstrate. Stern's method of argument is rare among social reformers: His call for greater job security is objective and non-sentimental. We should be particularly grateful that he makes his case without a single, modish reference to the Japanese experience with lifetime job security. (That we've had enough Japanese-inspired *mea culpas* is attested to by a joke currently making the rounds of business schools. A Frenchman, a Japanese, and an American are each sentenced to death and given one last wish. Says the Frenchman, "Let me sing the *Marseillaise* one last time before I die." Says the Japanese, "Let me give one last speech on the benefits of Japanese management practices." Says the American, "Shoot me before he gives that damn speech again.") Stern's method of argument is also rare among economists: As in the best of economics his analysis is data-oriented and based on actual experience. What is unusual is that he also includes research from *other* disciplines. While economics is no doubt the most useful of all the social sciences, economics *plus* any other discipline is even more useful. Stern combines what economists know about productivity with the findings of organizational theorists about worker motivation. This is the same combination that makes the writings of Herbert Simon and Lester Thurow so powerful and practical.

Stern starts his analysis with a review of the economic literature on worker productivity. He takes pains to consider the often conflicting research, and concludes that not only do workers have a significant impact on productivity, but labor productivity rises and falls inversely with job security.

During the troughs of the economic cycle, American industry lays off hundreds of thousands of workers. This system generates unemployment and welfare costs that must be paid by society, personal and familial costs that must be paid by workers, and rehiring and retraining costs that must be paid by employers. But there is also another cost that is frequently overlooked: Workers who are continually treated as the expendable factor of production come to develop a considerable antagonism toward their employers. Workers periodically thrown out of their jobs notice that the managers who have laid them off do not even take small cuts in their six-figure salaries (and, often, these managers vote dividends to stockholders while workers are in unemployment lines). As a consequence, when workers return to their jobs after a layoff they do so with reduced commitment to their employers and little respect for managers. Such workers are then given to support union demands for exorbitant wages and benefits as compensation for cyclical layoffs. In effect, the price industry pays for layoffs is excessive labor costs and a lack of employee loyalty. This translates into the high inflation and low productivity that characterize the auto, steel, and other heavy industries which make frequent use of long-term layoffs.

But it need not be thus. Significantly, there are a few American corporations that offer considerable job security to their employees (for example, IBM and Hewlett-Packard), and others that even offer contractual job guarantees (Lincoln Electric and Donnelly Mirrors). Most important, firms that offer job security are found not just in growing, non-cyclical industries: While competing successfully in the highly unpredictable women's fashion industry, the Olga company manages to avoid layoffs; while competing successfully in the cyclical auto parts industry, Fel-Pro has never laid a worker off in sixty-three years.

Certainly it would be unwise and impossible to provide every American worker with lifetime job security. (Here are three reasons: (1) Companies and entire industries must sometimes be allowed to go out of business; (2) labor mobility is a source of both personal freedom and economic efficiency; and (3) workers who goof off deserve to be fired). Nonetheless, American industry can do a far better job of planning for full employment than it does at present. Almost every company can schedule work more effectively to smooth out the effects of the business cycle, and almost all companies can enter into agreements with workers and unions for job sharing and reduced work weeks during recessions.

Significantly, workers at Donnelly, Lincoln, Olga, Fel-Pro, IBM, and Hewlett-Packard see that they have a commitment from the companies that employ them. In turn, this builds worker commitment to these companies. Workers in these firms understand that the welfare of their employers is inextricably tied to their own welfare. It is not surprising then to find that workers in these companies are engaged in efforts to increase productivity. Because they identify with company goals, workers in these firms are constantly on the lookout for ways to work more efficiently and effectively. To this end, managers provide mechanisms that permit workers to participate meaningfully in organizational decision making. These workers do not fear that by increasing their performance they will work their way out of their jobs. (Indeed, at Donnelly and Lincoln any worker who finds a way to eliminate his or her own job gets an automatic raise and a promotion!) Workers in these firms also share financially from gains in productivity. Thus, they are more than employees; they are partners in the enterprises where they work.

Now back to the apparent contradiction between the two sets of facts about security and productivity. Why is it that tenured teachers, professors, and civil servants don't act the same way as employees with job security in the private sector? The main reason is probably that teachers and public sector workers do not have the full responsibility for the quantity and quality of their work that is assumed by the private sector employees just described. Public sector employees do not participate meaningfully in decision making, and not at all in productivity gains. What this says is that job security is a necessary but not sufficient condition for employee commitment and productivity. What is also needed is an appropriate philosophy of management and an appropriate organization of work tasks. When working conditions are mismanaged, job security unfortunately can lead to employee irresponsibility. But when working conditions are well managed, security can become the catalyst for worker productivity.

This book suggests a positive, optimistic alternative future of work in which both the quantity and quality of jobs are increased. Stern's message is pro-business, pro-worker, pro-union, pro-productivity, pro–full employment, and pro–low inflation. Best of all, it shows that these interests are compatible and not in competition. Apparently, it is possible to resolve some of the terrible conundrums of economics.

JAMES O'TOOLE
University of Southern California
Los Angeles, November 1981

ACKNOWLEDGMENTS

Among the many people who have helped me, I would first like to thank Daniel Friedman. His encouragement supported my first efforts to write this all down. Other colleagues, friends, and mentors who contributed suggestions and information at various stages include Clayton Alderfer, Charles Benson, Guy Benveniste, David Berg, Gerald Duguay, Jacqueline Fralley, Mark Gerzon, Paul Goldfinger, Victor Gotbaum, Ellen Gould, Norton Grubb, Larry Hirshhorn, Richard Hackman, John Harter, Gary Hoachlander, Charles Lindblom, Raymond Miles, Joseph Pechman, James Rosenbaum, Eugene Sagan, Juanita Sagan, Daniel Smith, Robert Solow, Sarah Somers, Thomas Strano, Robert Stump, Jon Wagner and Mark Willis. In thanking these people, I must also admit that I did not always follow their advice.

Finally, I am happy to follow custom in expressing deep and lasting gratitude to my wife, Jane P. Stern, for all her encouragement and affection.

D.S.

CONTENTS

MANAGING HUMAN RESOURCES

Chapter 1

INTRODUCTION: THE ART OF FULL EMPLOYMENT

Remember full employment? The last time the U.S. economy approached it was 1973, when the unemployment rate was 4.9 percent. That was a prosperous year: After-tax per capita income (income to households from all sources, including dividends, interest, and other income from capital as well as wages and salaries) rose 6 percent faster than inflation.

In general, income per person has risen relatively fast in years with low unemployment. Figure 1.1 shows the average year-to-year changes in income for groups of years with similar unemployment rates. The lowest unemployment rates have occurred when war has taken large numbers of men out of the civilian labor force. The lowest unemployment rates attained in peacetime have been in the range of 4 to 4.9 percent. Figure 1.1 shows that these high-employment years on average have produced the most rapid growth in real disposable income per person. After taxes, income per person grew approximately 3.45 percent faster than inflation. When unemployment rates have been higher, growth in real purchasing power has been less.

The idea of full employment has long been associated with general prosperity. The Employment Act of 1946 directed the U.S. government "to promote maximum employment, production, and purchasing power." This commitment was reaffirmed by the 1978 Full Employment and Balanced Growth Act, which pledged the federal government to "promote full employment," among other things.

1

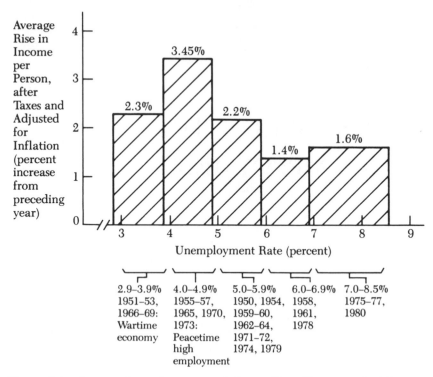

Figure 1.1   Average Unemployment and Year-to-Year Change in Real Disposable Income per Person in the U.S., 1950–1980. (*Sources:* Economic Report of the President 1981, *Table B-22.* Handbook of Labor Statistics, *1980, Table 28.*)

Sustaining Full Employment vs. Fighting Inflation

Yet in spite of the law, the 1970s had generally higher unemployment rates than the 1960s and 1950s. The reason, of course, was inflation. Promoting full employment seems to lead to increasing inflation, although economists disagree about how this happens. In any event, fighting inflation has had the result of increasing unemployment.

Some say the way to restore full employment without inflation is to cut government spending and taxes, encourage private investment, stop interfering with free enterprise, and maybe go back to a gold standard so that government will have less power to influence the supply of money. Others argue that the only way to have stable prices along with full employment is for the government to become *more* involved in the economy by imposing controls on wages and prices. Controls will work, they say, if supported by appropriate fiscal and monetary policies.

No one really knows how we can sustain full employment without accelerating inflation. Any theory has to rely on some conjecture and extrapolation from actual experience, because the history of the U.S. economy since the 1946 Employment Act has not provided a period of sustained full employment in peacetime without accelerating inflation. During one three-year stretch, 1955–1957, unemployment was less than 5 percent—but prices did accelerate, and a recession followed, raising unemployment to 6.8 percent in 1958.

Full Employment and Quality of Working Life

The theory I propose in this book is that sustaining full employment will become more feasible as the *quality* of employment improves. A growing number of employers, employees, and unions are now becoming involved in advancing what is often called the "quality of working life" (QWL). I see these efforts to improve QWL as part of a more general strategy to promote full employment. As it has evolved in actual practice, the general strategy appears to have three distinct elements. The first, which is most explicit in QWL efforts, is to make working conditions more agreeable to employees. One reason more employers are trying to anticipate and accommodate employees' personal wants is to prevent valued employees from quitting when alternative employment becomes available. A second element of the strategy, also intended to prevent the loss of valued employees, is the postponement of layoffs when business temporarily slows down. The third distinct part of the strategy is involvement of employees in determining how to increase productivity. Chapter 5 gives examples of all three parts of this strategy in use.

The purpose of this book is to explain how the separate parts of this strategy fit together and enhance each other. At present, various parts of the strategy are being adopted by various organizations for various reasons. Chapter 3 describes what I call an "emerging coalition" for full employment, productivity, and QWL. But the members of this coalition do not yet seem to be fully aware of what they have in common. This book is an effort to make the connections more apparent.

How Job Security Can Inhibit Productivity Growth—But Not Necessarily

The core of the theory is this: When the unemployment rate has been low for a while, productivity growth tends to slow down (see Chapter 2). Costs and prices then tend to rise. One reason productivity growth slows down is that quit rates go up, so more new people have to be trained quickly. Mistakes, delays, and waste become more frequent. Also, both the rise in quit rates and the slowdown in productivity growth are symptoms of what I call the "job security effect": When jobs are plentiful and employees have attractive alternatives available, it becomes more costly for managers and supervisors to enforce demands for the extra efforts that are occasionally (or often) required to keep a productive operation going. Firing people is less feasible when turnover is already high. Employees may become less willing to comply with extra demands, and if confrontations occur they are in a better position to quit.

When unemployment rates go back up—as they always have done—quit rates go back down. Firing or demoting an employee who does not perform becomes more feasible. The implicit threat of dismissal or layoff becomes more credible, and employees may become more willing to comply with extra demands when other jobs are less readily available. Employees may also try to restrict output at such times in order to make it look as if they are still busy, but this will not prevent layoffs if sales have declined and are not expected to rebound soon. After a wave of layoffs has raised the unemployment rate, productivity starts to grow faster again.

Replacing trained employees can be expensive, whether they have quit or been fired or laid off. To counter the job security effect and high quit rates when the economy is near full employment, some companies have been evolving ways to manage human resources without relying on the implicit threat of dismissal or demotion to keep employees motivated. Instead they rely on an increased sense of responsibility and personal motivation on the part of employees. Job enrichment, Scanlon plans, quality circles, and many QWL programs all try to cultivate this sense of personal responsibility. In return, employees may be paid cash bonuses when productivity improves, as in a Scanlon plan. Or they may receive some explicit commitment that their job security will be protected. Or there may be a variety of improvements in QWL, which will help deter valued employees from quitting when alternative employment opportunities become available.

As more employers and employees discover how to reconcile job security with rapid growth in productivity, it becomes more feasible to sustain full employment in the economy as a whole. Reducing the job security effect prevents some of the slowdown in productivity growth that has, historically, caused costs and prices to rise when unemployment rates have been kept down. (Chapter 2 explains this argument in more detail.) For an employer, the payoff from reducing the job security effect comes when business is brisk and the unemployment rate is low. At these times organizations that can keep people motivated and avoid quits will have a competitive advantage. Conversely, strategies to strengthen personal motivation and stabilize employment are most costly when business slows down, because postponing layoffs is expensive. Therefore, as Chapter 3 describes, a high-employment economy is more favorable for investment in efforts to reduce the job security effect.

One clear implication for national economic policy is that keeping unemployment rates low in the short run will make it more feasible to sustain full employment in the long run. Low unemployment rates in the short run give an advantage to employers that have adopted a management strategy consistent with full employment. Such employers will tend to expand, and others will either follow suit or suffer eventual reductions in market share.

In addition to keeping unemployment down in the short run, which is something the federal government can do, there are various ways in which governments at all levels can promote full employment, productivity, and QWL. As employers themselves, governments are in the best position to demonstrate tactics for reducing the job security effect—since civil service gives government employees more job security than most employees in the private sector. For example, one idea that has great appeal to civil service employees, and could have wide applicability in the private sector as long-term employment becomes the norm, is paid sabbatical leave. This and other ideas are presented in Chapter 4.

Other Factors: Physical Capital and Personal Ideals

Except for a brief discussion of pension funds as a possible source of financing for sabbaticals, I say very little in this book about capital or investment. The focus is on the management of human resources, not on the management, design, or acquisition of physical or financial assets. Economists generally have put more emphasis on physical capital accumulation as a requirement for raising productivity and attaining full employment. This book may serve as a reminder that human factors are also important. A complete theory of full employment would have to consider both sets of factors. One or two of the companies mentioned in this book have made progress in combining capital planning with improvement of QWL. The theory of "socio-technical systems," however, still has more to say to human resource managers than to finance managers.

Another limitation of this book is that it provides no estimate of how much time it would take for the recommended strategies to work, were they fully adopted. The recommendations are therefore susceptible to attack on the grounds that any investment required is hard to justify when the outcome is so uncertain.

Still, employers and employees in both the private and public sector have been engaging in costly efforts to improve QWL along with productivity. Where unions exist, they have increasingly acted as full collaborators in these efforts. These efforts have been undertaken mainly because they are considered good for business as well as for employees. Some of the innovating managers, unionists, and employees have also expressed an idealistic interest in making work more like what they think it should be. "Quality of working life" has an ethical appeal in addition to its economic value for an individual organization or for the economy as a whole.

One of my own favorite statements about the quality of working life was published in 1923, long before "QWL" was conceived, by American philosopher John Dewey. I have found it useful in imagining what the never-yet-achieved state of sustained full employment may be like.

> *It is important not to confuse the psychological distinction between play and work with the economic distinction. Psychologically, the defining characteristic of play is not amusement nor aimlessness. It is the fact that the aim is thought of as more activity in the same line, without defining continuity of action in reference to results produced. Activities as they grow more complicated gain added meaning by greater attention to specific results achieved. Thus they pass gradually into work.* Both are equally free and intrinsically motivated, *apart from false economic conditions which tend to make play into idle excitement for the well to do, and work into uncongenial labor for the poor. Work*

is psychologically simply an activity which consciously includes regard for consequences as a part of itself; it becomes constrained labor when the consequences are outside of the activity as an end to which activity is merely a means. Work which remains permeated with the play attitude is art—in quality if not in conventional designation. (Dewey, pp. 241–242; emphasis added.)

Chapter 2

HOW GOOD JOBS CAN HELP SUSTAIN FULL EMPLOYMENT

Creating more intrinsically motivating work will make it more feasible to sustain full employment. Management strategies designed to elicit intrinsic motivation can avoid some of the slowdown in productivity growth that otherwise tends to occur when unemployment rates stay low for a while. This tendency has been noted by many observers of the U.S. economy, some of whom have also attributed it to what I am calling the "job security effect." Reducing the job security effect permits economic expansion and low unemployment to continue longer by avoiding or delaying the upward pressure on costs and prices that occurs when productivity growth slows down.

The job security effect apparently helps explain the slower rate of productivity growth in the 1970s, which added to inflationary pressure and made it more difficult to sustain full employment. The year 1974 was particularly bad—productivity actually fell sharply, rather than rising as usual. In fact, a large part of the decline in productivity growth in the 1970s occurred in 1974 alone. Edward Denison, a leading analyst of productivity trends, called 1974 a "mystery." Other experts agreed. But the drop in productivity came just after a period of unprecedented conditions in the labor market that had given employees a great deal of opportunity and choice relative to employers. The behavior of productivity in 1974 was therefore consistent with the usual operation of the job security effect. When this effect is taken into account, the slowdown in productivity growth in the 1970s appears much less mysterious. This argument is presented in more detail later in this chapter.

The job security effect is not the only possible explanation for the productivity drop of 1974. Martin N. Baily has argued that the sudden rise in oil prices in 1973 made part of the nation's stock of productive capital economically obsolete, as indicated by the market value of corporate equity. Standard methods of analyzing productivity trends did not take this into account. Premature obsolescence of the capital stock due to the oil price shock therefore can also explain some of the "mystery" of 1974. Most likely, both oil prices and the job security effect played a part, with varied relative importance among different industries and among firms within an industry.

That the job security effect generally does play some part is indicated not only by data for the economy at large, but also by case studies of individual companies. This chapter contains summaries of two well-publicized cases: American Telephone and Telegraph and Donnelly Mirrors. Both provide evidence that management strategies designed to enhance employees' intrinsic motivation have been able to offset the job security effect in times of low unemployment. If such strategies were used by more employers, low unemployment rates could be maintained longer.

Why Full Employment?

Low unemployment rates have been accompanied by bigger average increases in after-tax, constant-dollar income per person, as Figure 1.1 showed. Conversely, high unemployment rates are associated with various kinds of stress, crime, illness, and even death. For instance, a married couple is more likely to break up if a breadwinner has become unemployed (Ross and Sawhill, 1975). Father's unemployment is also "the variable that shows up most frequently as somehow related to child abuse" in the records of social agencies dealing with that problem. "This finding confirms a widely held theory that family stress, both emotional and financial, related to unemployment, ties into incidence of abuse" (Light, 1973, p. 588). For reasons like these, the Carnegie Council on Children declared,

> [We] *support above all national policies to help equalize the impact of economic forces on our entire citizenry. This will take a commitment to creating jobs and achieving full employment, so that no American child will suffer because a parent cannot find work or earn enough to provide a decent living.* (Keniston, p. 79)

Of course, marital separations and child abuse would not disappear even if unemployment were entirely eliminated. For some individuals, both unemployment and family problems may be symptomatic of personal difficulties. Reducing unemployment will not solve all family problems, but it is likely to prevent some. Reducing unemployment is also likely to prevent some suicides, homicides, admissions to state mental hospitals and prisons, and deaths from cirrhosis of the liver, heart and kidney disease, and certain other causes. The relationship between unemployment rates and these seven measures of stress-related pathology has been established by Harvey Brenner. In a report to the U.S. Congress Joint Economic Committee, Brenner examined the relationship over time between each of these seven measures and the rate of unemployment, as well as the rate of price inflation and the level of per capita income. For the period from World War II to 1973 (more or less), using separate sets of annual data for the United States as a whole, England and Wales, Sweden, and the states of New York, Massachusetts, and California, Brenner found:

> *Overall, the data showed that the association between the* unemployment rate *and all the pathological indices was statistically significant. Consistency was also shown in these relationships across age, sex, and racial groups, among different states, and for three different countries.*
>
> *Relationships between the* inflation rate *and pathological indices were often statistically significant, but often quite inconsistent from one of the pathological indices to another, among countries. The chronic disease mortality, in particular, did not appear to show significant relationships with the inflation rate, while suicide, homicide, and imprisonment did.*
>
> Per capita income *showed its most important and easily interpretable inverse relationships in connection with total mortality by age and sex for the three countries and three states. Positive relationships between per capita income and several of the measures of pathology (e.g., suicide, homicide, and imprisonment) were less easy to understand.* (Brenner, 1976, pp. 89–90)

Since these findings are merely correlations, not the results of controlled experiments, Brenner expressly disavowed any inference of causality. The most he would say is that "serious, if not vital, national concerns tend to be associated with economic processes" (p. 7).

No such methodological scruples inhibited the Chairman of the Joint Economic Committee at the time, Senator Hubert Humphrey. In a dramatically worded letter of transmittal, Humphrey used

Brenner's findings to claim that the 1.4 percent rise in the unemployment rate in 1970, which has been sustained since then, was "directly responsible for some 51,570 total deaths." This includes 26,440 deaths from heart and kidney disease which "are directly attributable to the rise in unemployment during 1970." Humphrey went on to say,

> . . . *the federal government knows how to minimize unemployment. It knows how to reduce it using monetary and fiscal policy and to keep it down. This study, for the first time, offers our government the capability to accurately and fully measure the impact of these economic policies. Economic policy planners can and will now know the full and tragic cost of unemployment if they fail to hold it at a minimum.*
> (Brenner, p. ix)

Full Employment Promised by Law

After Hubert Humphrey's death, Congress passed the Humphrey-Hawkins Act, officially entitled the Full Employment and Balanced Growth Act of 1978. In the list of findings at the beginning, Congress stated,

> *Unemployment exposes many families to social, psychological, and physiological costs, including disruption of family life, loss of individual dignity and self-respect, and the aggravation of physical and psychological illnesses, alcoholism and drug abuse, crime, and social conflicts.* (P.L. 95-523, sec. 2(a) (5))

The 1978 Full Employment Act then reaffirmed and elaborated the purposes of the Employment Act of 1946.

The 1946 Employment Act was passed early in the first session of Congress to convene after World War II. In three pages it established the purpose and procedure for setting national economic policy. It created the President's Council of Economic Advisors, which became an official platform for the economics profession. The 1946 Act pronounced its declaration of policy:

> *The Congress hereby declares that it is the continuing policy and responsibility of the federal government to use all practicable means consistent with its needs and obligations and other essential considerations of national policy, with the assistance and cooperation of industry, agriculture, labor, and state and local governments, to coordinate and utilize all its plans, functions, and resources for the purpose of creating and maintaining, in a manner calculated to foster and promote free competitive enterprise and the general welfare, con-*

ditions under which there will be afforded useful employment opportunities, including self-employment, for those able, willing, and seeking to work, and to promote maximum employment, production, and purchasing power. (P.L. 79-304, sec. 2)

In the 1978 Act, this statement of purpose was preserved virtually as it had stood for 32 years, but even more words were added. Instead of "maximum employment, production, and purchasing power," the last clause became:

. . . and promote full employment and production, increased real income, balanced growth, a balanced federal budget, adequate productivity growth, proper attention to national priorities, achievement of an improved trade balance through increased exports and improvement in the international competitiveness of agriculture, business, and industry, and reasonable price stability . . . (P.L. 95-523, sec. 102)

In addition, the 1978 declaration of policy included another nine subsections, so the statement of purpose that took 12 lines in 1946 now took two full pages of small print. (The whole 1978 Act is 22 pages long, compared to 3 pages in 1946.) This makes it difficult, if not impossible, to define concisely and accurately what the purpose of national economic policy is. In contrast to "maximum employment, production, and purchasing power," the stated objectives of policy in the 1978 Act lacked both cadence and coherence.

Still, this Act gave top priority to reducing unemployment. It stated that the goal for unemployment in 1983 should be not more than 3 percent among individuals aged 20 and over, and 4 percent overall. (It required that unemployment rates continue to be computed by the same procedure used in 1978.) And, while also setting a 1983 goal of a 3 percent inflation rate, it stipulated that "policies and procedures for reducing the rate of inflation shall be designed so as not to impede achievement of the goals and timetables . . . for the reduction of unemployment" (P.L. 95-523, sec. 4). The promise of full employment is clearly stated by law. But this promise has become increasingly difficult to fulfill in reality.

Unemployment and Inflation

The Humphrey-Hawkins Act set a goal of 4 percent overall unemployment for 1983. Why 4 percent? Why not 3, 6, or 0? What is "full employment," exactly?

Full Employment as Defined by Economists

A straightforward definition of full employment would be the availability of a job for everyone. Whenever a shop or factory or office has to let people go for some reason, there should be other jobs open for those laid-off workers to find. When students finish their schooling and start looking for full-time work, or when parents who have been busy with child care decide to seek paid jobs outside the home, there should be jobs available. In other words, the number of job openings should at least equal the number of people looking for work. This definition of full employment was advocated by the influential British economist, Sir William Beveridge, in the 1940s.

Despite its appeal to common sense, Beveridge's definition did not prevail. To put it into practice would require keeping track of two things: the number of people seeking work, and the number of job openings. Economists have pointed to the difficulties in getting an accurate count of job openings. For instance, is there really an opening if the pay being offered is too low to attract anyone? Again, similar difficulties arise in counting unemployed people. Should someone be considered unemployed if he or she is holding out for a salary that is unrealistically high? However, such difficulties do not prevent the collection and publication of statistics on unemployment.

What prevented the adoption of Beveridge's definition, at least in this country, was not the difficulty of counting job vacancies. It was the failure of that definition to incorporate a concern for preventing inflation. The prevailing view among American economists since World War II has been that pushing unemployment down too far will cause prices to rise too fast. Exactly how far down is "too far" is a question economists have debated long and hard. Despite strong disagreement about how low the unemployment rate can or should be, there has been general agreement that it depends on the danger of inflation. To urge that the unemployment rate should simply be no greater than the job vacancy rate ignores this danger.

Changes in Rates of Unemployment and Inflation Since 1950

Perceptions of where the inflationary danger arises have changed over time as economic conditions themselves have changed. Figure 2.1 provides a convenient visual history of inflation and unemployment in the United States from 1950 though 1980. Inflation is measured vertically, unemployment horizontally. Each point shows the

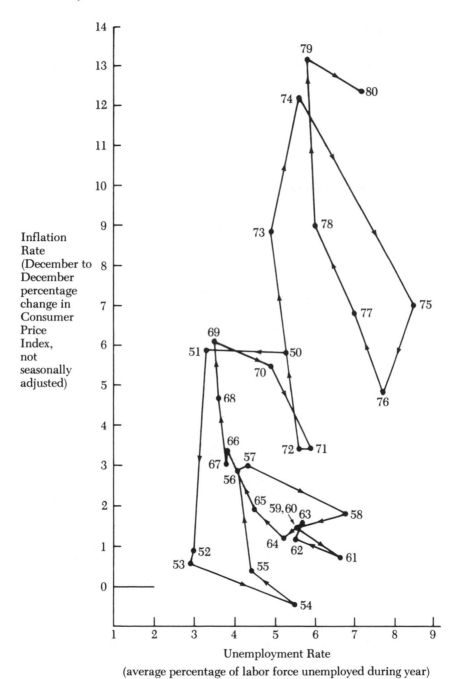

Figure 2.1 Inflation and Unemployment Rates by Year, 1950–1980. (*Sources:* Economic Report of the President, 1981, *Tables B-29 and B-53; updated with Bureau of Labor Statistics news release, "The Consumer Price Index—December 1980."*)

combination of inflation and unemployment in one year; the last two numbers of the year are written next to each point. Arrows on the lines between the points show the direction of time. We can see, for example, that from 1961 to 1969 the economy followed a fairly smooth, curved path upward and to the left. Along this path unemployment decreased while the rate of inflation increased, and year-to-year increases in inflation got bigger while year-to-year decreases in unemployment got smaller. In other words, as the 1960s progressed, the inflationary danger of further reductions in unemployment became more evident.

An Optimistic Projection from the 1960s

In 1967 the distinguished American labor economist, Robert Aaron Gordon, published a book entitled *The Goal of Full Employment*. This was the culmination of a research project supported by the Ford Foundation, with the goals of defining full employment and designing policies to achieve it. Based on data through 1965 and assuming the implementation of effective programs to train groups with chronically high rates of unemployment, Gordon proposed a "full employment goal corresponding to a national unemployment rate of about 3 percent." He guessed that "within the next decade . . . it might be possible to maintain unemployment at 3 percent with an inflationary price trend of perhaps 1.5–2.5 percent" (p. 182).

Like other predictions of the 1960s, this turned out to be overly optimistic. Figure 2.1 shows that the U.S. economy followed a path from 1976 through 1979 that was similar in shape to the 1961–1969 path, moving upward and to the left. But the more recent sequence took place at drastically higher rates of inflation *and* unemployment. A decade after Gordon published his hopeful guess, the unemployment rate was more than twice as high as his proposed target, and the rate of inflation was about four times faster than what he hoped would occur at full employment!

The Carter Administration's Retreat from the Humphrey-Hawkins Goals

When the Carter Administration took office in the first quarter of 1977, unemployment was 7.4 percent, and consumer prices in 1976 had risen 4.8 percent. By the end of 1978, unemployment had been brought down to 5.9 percent—but the rate of inflation had again accelerated. The Economic Report of the President in January, 1979—the first to be issued after the passage of the Humphrey-Hawkins bill—therefore began, "First, reducing inflation must be our top economic priority" (p. 3). On its face, this statement directly contradicts the Humphrey-Hawkins provision that anti-inflation policies must not impede achievement of employment goals. Even though the overall unemployment rate was still nearly 6 percent— far from the Humphrey-Hawkins target of 4 percent—national economic policy was forced to deal first with raging inflation.

Despite the priority given to fighting inflation in 1979, inflation won. In his next economic report to the Congress, in January 1980—an election year—Democratic President Carter was forced explicitly to revise the Humphrey-Hawkins goals:

> *In 1978 the Humphrey-Hawkins Full Employment and Balanced Growth Act was passed with the active support of my Administration. The general objectives of the act—and those of my Administration— are to achieve full employment and reasonable price stability.*
>
> *When I signed that act a little over a year ago, it was my hope that we could achieve by 1983 the interim goals it set forth: to reduce the overall unemployment rate to 4 percent and to achieve a 3 percent inflation rate.*
>
> *Since the end of 1978, however, huge OPEC oil price increases have made the outlook for economic growth much worse, and at the same time have sharply increased inflation. The economic policies I have recommended for the next 2 years will help the economy adjust to the impact of higher OPEC oil prices. But no policies can change the realities which those higher prices impose.*
>
> *I have therefore been forced to conclude that reaching the goals of a 4 percent unemployment rate and 3 percent inflation by 1983 is no longer practicable. Reduction of the unemployment rate to 4 percent by 1983, starting from the level now expected in 1981, would require an extraordinary high economic growth rate. Efforts to stimulate the economy to achieve so high a growth rate would be counterproductive. The immediate result would be extremely strong upward pressure on wage rates, costs, and prices. This would undercut the basis for sustained economic expansion and postpone still further the date at which we could reasonably expect a return to a 4 percent unemployment rate.*
>
> *Reducing inflation from the 10 percent expected in 1980 to 3 percent by 1983 would be an equally unrealistic expectation. Recent experience indicates that the momentum of inflation built up over the past 15 years is extremely strong. A practical goal for reducing inflation must take this fact into account.*
>
> *Because of these economic realities, I have used the authority provided to me in the Humphrey-Hawkins Act to extend the timetable for*

achieving a 4 percent unemployment rate and 3 percent inflation. The target year for achieving 4 percent unemployment is now 1985, a 2-year deferment. The target year for lowering inflation to 3 percent has been postponed until 3 years after that. (pp. 9–10)

A year later the election was over. Voters' dissatisfaction with the economy had contributed to Carter's defeat. Just before leaving office, in January 1981, the Carter Administration published its last economic report. Again the timetable for complying with Humphrey-Hawkins had to be pushed back. This time the revision of goals was not mentioned in the President's message itself. It appeared in the middle of the accompanying report of the Council of Economic Advisers, just before an appendix on revision of the National Income and Product Accounts. The Council's new projections for inflation and unemployment, along with its projections from the preceding year, are shown in Table 2.1. Not only are the more recent projections higher for both inflation and unemployment, the Humphrey-Hawkins targets are no longer seen as attainable even on the horizon. All we can hope for in 1985, according to the 1981 Council, is to be about where we were in 1977. In Figure 2.1 this does not look very good.

A "Natural Rate" of Unemployment?

For a few economists, this history of ever-receding goals, however regrettable, is not surprising. Milton Friedman is the best known of the small number in the 1960s who expressed doubt about the government's ability to reduce unemployment. In his presidential address to the American Economic Association, published in 1968, Friedman argued that there is a "natural" rate of unemployment determined by the classical theory of supply and demand. That is, if employing another worker adds less to total output than the average output per worker already employed, total employment should tend toward that level where the value of the last worker's output equals the real (price-adjusted) wage. This would be the "natural" level of employment. But since there are always some people between jobs or just entering the labor market, there would also be some "natural" unemployment. If the government followed an expansionary policy in order to reduce unemployment below the natural rate, it would have to let prices go up faster than money wages, so that the real wage falls and employers' demand for workers will

Table 2.1 **Projections of Unemployment and Inflation Rates, January 1980 and January 1981**

	1981	1982	1983	1984	1985
Unemployment rate (percent, fourth quarter, seasonally adjusted)					
1980 projection	7.3	6.5	5.6	4.8	4.0
1981 projection	7.7	7.4	7.0	6.6	6.2
Inflation rate (percent increase in Consumer Price Index, fourth quarter to fourth quarter)					
1980 projection	8.7	7.9	7.2	6.5	5.8
1981 projection	12.6	9.6	8.2	7.5	6.7

SOURCES: *Annual Report of the Council of Economic Advisers,* January 1980, p. 94; January 1981, p. 178.

increase. But as soon as workers realize that prices are rising faster than money wages, they will demand that money wages rise more rapidly. Then the government has to provide more stimulus so that prices rise faster still—in order to keep the real wage down so that unemployment stays below its natural rate. Friedman concluded, "There is always a temporary trade-off between inflation and unemployment; there is no permanent trade-off" (p. 11). Keeping unemployment below the natural rate requires continually *accelerating* inflation. A constant rate of inflation, even a high rate, will not do the trick.

Looking again at the curve from 1961 through 1969 in Figure 2.1, there does appear to be some confirmation of this "accelerationist" theory, as it came to be called. Smaller and smaller annual decreases in the rate of unemployment seem to require bigger and bigger rates of inflation. Writing about two thirds of the way through this stretch of history, Friedman can be credited with an accurate prediction for the remaining one third.

But does the "natural rate" theory explain the 1970s? If inflation accelerated when unemployment went below 4 percent in the late 1960s, why did it accelerate again in 1972–1974 when the unemployment rate was more than 5 percent? And then again in 1976–1979, when unemployment was 6 to 7 percent? Friedman himself acknowledged in 1968,

Unfortunately, we have as yet devised no method to estimate accurately and readily the natural rate of either interest or unemployment. And the "natural" rate will itself change from time to time. (p. 10)

Friedman says the government should not even concern itself with discovering what the natural rate is. Government should stop trying to make the actual unemployment rate equal the natural rate or any other rate. Government should just reduce its own spending, keep the money supply growing at a steady, pre-announced rate, and let the private economy settle where it will. Even if the "natural" rate of unemployment were known, attempts by government to make the actual rate equal the natural rate would be destabilizing and counterproductive.

Since Friedman's 1968 article, other economists have elaborated and reinforced these ideas in theoretical and empirical models of the economy. In 1968 Edmund Phelps published an analysis leading to conclusions similar to Friedman's. Prominent among more recent contributors to this line of work are Robert E. Lucas, Jr. and Thomas Sargent. What unifies this "new classical" school of macroeconomics, as their Keynesian counterparts call them, is precisely their rejection of the active, discretionary style of policy associated with Keynesian theory. According to Lucas, one of the "findings" of "new classical" research

. . . is that what had formerly been accepted as evidence that economists do know how to fine tune the economy through monetary and fiscal policies (namely, the empirical success of Keynesian econometric models) is no evidence at all. The multipliers we use in advising heads of state are meaningless numbers, just as were the trade-offs we offered our fellow-citizens a decade ago. (Lucas, 1981, p. 563)

Instead of trying to design today's monetary and fiscal policy according to today's economic conditions, Lucas urges economists to adopt the more "honest" and limited role of formulating *rules* for the government itself to follow—so that businesses and households, knowing these rules in advance, can conduct their affairs without the uncertainty of ever-changing government policies.

With the 1980 Presidential election, "new classical macroeconomics" appears to have prevailed. Milton and Rose Friedman's book *Free to Choose* was at the top of the best-seller list during the election year, and it was the basis for a TV series. Ronald Reagan called it "superb." The Reagan Administration immediately adopted a "new classical" program of reduced spending, steady and moderate growth of the money supply at a pre-announced rate, and a pre-announced series of tax reductions. These policies are intended to reduce both inflation *and* unemployment. No trade-off is considered necessary.

Neo-Classical vs. Neo-Keynesian Arguments

But within the economics profession a vehement debate continues. Neo-Keynesians like James Tobin, Alan Blinder, and the late Arthur Okun have argued that the government should not surrender its discretion over fiscal and monetary policy. Their analysis continues to rely on the theory that year-to-year decreases in inflation will tend to be accompanied by increases in unemployment, and vice versa. They are agnostic about whether this trade-off between inflation and unemployment disappears in the long run, as the "natural rate" hypothesis asserts.

One can argue that the spiral in Figure 2.1 has resulted in part from an upward drift in the "natural rate" of unemployment. Various explanations for such a drift have been proposed. Tobin puts these explanations in three categories. First, demographic: The labor force in the 1970s included growing proportions of women and young people, who are "more prone to spells of unemployment" than are prime-aged males. Tobin notes, on the other hand, that rising levels of educational attainment and stronger attachment of women to paid work would have the opposite effect. Second, government policies: Unemployment compensation and welfare benefits have made unemployment more tolerable and may have encouraged people to stay unemployed longer. But here Tobin observes that changes in these programs have usually followed rises in unemployment, rather than preceded them, so it is difficult to see how they could have *caused* unemployment to increase. Third, less productive capacity relative to the labor force: Given a prolonged period of slack demand, businesses may not have maintained enough productive equipment and facilities to keep the labor force fully employed. This argument will be mentioned again on the following pages as an explanation for declining productivity growth. But Tobin concludes that these three sets of historical developments do not add up to an explanation of why the "natural rate" of unemployment should have risen from 4 percent to 6 or 7 percent, or whatever it may be. To say that the combination of higher unemployment *and* inflation is due to a rise in the natural rate of unemployment "merely describes but does not explain the chronic acceleration of inflation itself" (Tobin, 1980, p. 60).

Neo-Keynesian Explanations of Inflation in the 1970s

Neo-Keynesians do not attribute the higher inflation rates of the 1970s to a rise in some unobservable "natural" rate of unemployment. They insist that government can and should use flexible monetary and fiscal policies to avoid high rates of unemployment. Their explanation for the inflation of the 1970s begins with the excessively stimulating fiscal policy of the mid-1960s: Federal spending for the Vietnam war and domestic programs was financed by borrowing rather than through taxes. Political motives may also account for the excessively stimulating monetary and fiscal policies that preceded the 1972 Presidential election. The rise in prices of food, fuel, and other commodities in 1972–1974 and 1978–1979 were due to OPEC, bad harvests, and other misfortunes that the government could not control. These events all appear as sharp upward movements in Figure 2.1.

Once such "shocks" have occurred, they tend to be incorporated into the "underlying" inflationary process. Barry Bosworth, who headed the Council on Wage and Price Stability in the Carter Administration, describes this as

> . . . a self-perpetuating underlying cycle of wage and price inflation that is only loosely related to overall demand conditions and may be more reflective of the fact that inflation has existed in the past and that everyone expects it to continue . . . . (Bosworth, 1981, p. 61)

An important question is whether this underlying process would, in the absence of any "shocks," just keep wages and prices rising at a constant rate, or whether it would accelerate. James Tobin has suggested that there is a tendency toward acceleration because job vacancies and unfilled orders cause wages and prices to rise more than job applicants and unsold inventories cause them to fall. This hypothesis has led Tobin to conclude that some kind of wage and price controls are needed, in addition to a deflationary monetary and fiscal policy, to bring inflation down. Some neo-Keynesians have developed ingenious proposals for "tax-based incomes policies" (Okun and Perry, 1978). However, other neo-Keynesians, notably Alan Blinder, have strongly opposed any kind of controls.

Other Complications, and the Search for Acceptable Solutions

No one can accuse the economics profession of trying to make things seem simpler than they are! The foregoing account only summarizes the major controversies. There have also been discussions about whether the unemployment statistics themselves are less accurate than they used to be. Some have suggested that employment has grown faster in the "underground economy" than in the tax-paying, record-keeping establishments from which public statistics are compiled. In addition to the traditional criminal sector, "underground" employment includes illegal aliens and individuals who exchange legal goods and services through barter rather than receive payment in cash. Any such rise in uncounted employment could be said to cause an increase in the "natural rate" of unemployment.

Are we left, then, with a choice between submitting to some high and rising "natural rate" of unemployment—and paying the toll in stress, crime, disease, and death—or subjecting ourselves to some bureaucratic system of wage and price controls? Do we need a war, or some moral equivalent, to make it possible for everyone to find a job and still know what the money earned in wages or salary is really worth? This frightening possibility could lend urgency to a search for more appealing alternatives. Some of these alternatives consist of new strategies for increasing economic productivity.

Inflation and Slower Growth in Productivity

Anything that causes inflation to accelerate makes it more difficult to achieve full employment, because national monetary and fiscal policies designed to reduce inflation have the immediate effect of reducing the overall amount of economic activity and therefore increasing unemployment. In spite of the explicit provisions of the 1978 Full Employment and Balanced Growth Act that full employment policies should take precedence over anti-inflation policies, the fact is that if something causes higher inflation it will usually trigger policies which create higher unemployment, at least temporarily.

Lower rates of productivity growth have been an important cause of accelerating inflation in the 1970s, and have therefore made it more difficult to fulfill the promise of full employment. The 1979 Economic Report of the President explained,

A large part of the worsening of inflation [in 1978] . . . stemmed from poor productivity. Over the past decade or more, the rate of growth in our productivity has been slowing. In late 1977 and throughout 1978, the slowdown in productivity growth reached serious proportions. Last year the productivity of our economy increased by less than 1 percent.

The reasons for the weakening of productivity growth in our country, especially its poor performance last year, are complex and are not fully understood. But the consequences are well known. With slower productivity growth, our living standards individually and as a Nation cannot rise as fast. Slower productivity growth means that . . . large increases in wages and other incomes put greater upward pressure on costs and prices. If we ignore the realities of slower productivity growth–if governments continue to press forward with unabated claims on resources, and private citizens continue to demand large gains in money incomes–our inflationary problem will worsen. (p. 6)

Similarly, the Chairman of the Federal Reserve Board warned in 1978,

Unless the economy's productivity expands at a faster rate, we will be unable to reduce unemployment without igniting inflation. Increased productivity is the best prospect for breaking the vicious cycle of wages chasing prices and prices chasing wages. (Miller, pp. 1–2)

The 1981 report of the Council of Economic Advisers elaborated on this problem:

Advances in productivity are the foundation of advances in our standard of living. Increases in output per worker lead to increases in real income. . . . Thus, when productivity growth declines, these other advances also are delayed. But expectations of a rising living standard persist. They perpetuate demands for real income gains which can no longer be met and which lead to inflationary increases in wages. . . . Since the mid-1960s, the growth rate of labor productivity has been declining from its postwar highs. In recent years the decline has been so marked as to pose a major challenge to public policy. Because declining productivity growth brings with it prospects for slower improvement in our standard of living and contributes to inflation, a program to stimulate productivity growth must be a keystone of economic policy. (pp. 68–69)

Average Productivity of Labor

Productivity is generally defined as the amount of output per unit of some input. The simplest measure of productivity is output per employee. Another is output per employee-hour, computed by dividing total output by total paid hours. These are both measures of what is properly called average productivity of labor. But changes in average productivity of labor are caused not only by changes in the characteristics or behavior of employees. The U.S. Bureau of Labor Statistics, which is the main source of data on average productivity of labor, attaches a routine disclaimer that these data

> *do not measure the specific contributions of labor, capital, or any other single factor of production. Rather, they reflect the joint effects of many influences, including new technology, capital investment, the level of output, capacity utilization, energy use, and managerial skills, as well as the skills and efforts of the work force.*

Average productivity of labor is a useful concept because the revenues from a business enterprise, apart from taxes and cost of materials, become income either for its employees or for its owners and creditors. If the average productivity of labor does not change, then any rise in wages or salaries for employees must reduce the income of owners and creditors—unless the enterprise's product can be sold at a higher price. But if average productivity of labor increases, wages or salaries of employees can increase without requiring either a reduction in owners' income or a rise in prices. A decline in the rate of growth of average labor productivity therefore puts more pressure on business to raise prices to offset rising wages and salaries.

The Productivity Puzzle

Table 2.2 shows the percentage change in various measures of average labor productivity in the United States each year from 1948 to 1978 or 1980. The first column shows percentage changes in a measure constructed by Edward Denison, who has done the most complete analysis of American economic growth. Denison uses a measure of real output per employee. The next three columns show percentage changes in real output per employee-hour, as reported by the U.S. Bureau of Labor Statistics. Despite these differences in

Table 2.2   Average Labor Productivity: Percentage Change from Preceding Year, Selected Measures, 1948–1980

Year	*(1)* National Income per Person Employed, Nonresidential Business Sector	U.S. Bureau of Labor Statistics Output per Hour of All Persons		
		(2) Private Business Total	*(3)* Non-Farm Business	*(4)* Manufacturing
1948	3.0	5.3	4.3	6.5
49	0.2	1.5	2.0	3.7
1950	7.5	7.9	6.0	5.7
51	2.2	2.8	1.7	3.2
52	1.7	3.2	2.3	1.8
53	2.6	3.2	1.7	1.8
54	0.2	1.6	1.4	1.6
55	6.6	4.0	3.9	5.0
56	0.7	1.0	0.3	−0.7
57	1.0	2.5	1.7	2.0
58	0.7	3.1	2.4	−0.5
59	5.8	1.6	1.6	4.7
1960	0.8	3.1	2.5	1.0
61	2.0	3.3	2.9	2.4
62	5.3	3.8	3.6	4.6
63	4.0	3.7	3.2	7.1
64	4.1	4.3	3.9	5.2
65	4.4	3.5	3.1	3.3
66	2.0	3.1	2.5	1.4
67	0.0	2.2	1.9	0.3
68	3.0	3.3	3.3	3.6
69	−0.3	0.2	−0.3	1.2
1970	−0.5	0.9	0.3	−0.3
71	2.8	3.6	3.3	5.4
72	4.1	3.5	3.7	5.1
73	1.1	2.7	2.5	2.7
74	−4.9	−2.3	−2.4	−5.2
75	−0.7	2.3	2.1	5.0
76	4.2	3.3	3.2	4.4
77	1.4	2.1	2.0	3.1
78	0.2	−0.2	−0.2	0.6
79		−0.4	−0.8	1.1
1980				−0.3

SOURCES: Column (1), Denison, 1979, Table 2-7; columns (2) and (3), *Economic Report of the President*, 1981, Table B-39; column (4), for 1948–1959, U.S. Bureau of Labor Statistics *Handbook of Labor Statistics*, 1978, Table 79, for 1960–1978, U.S. Bureau of Labor Statistics *Handbook of Labor Statistics*, 1980, Table 103, and for 1979 and 1980, U.S. Bureau of Labor Statistics news release *Productivity and Costs*, July 30, 1981, Table 4 and Appendix Table 4.

the way "labor" is measured, and in spite of differences in the scope of the economic sector for which output is counted, these four columns of Table 2.2 all show some things in common. Rates of change in all these measures of average labor productivity were generally lower from 1966 through 1970 than they were from 1948 through 1965. There were some bad years before 1966, and 1968 was a good year, but the period from 1966 through 1970 stands out as a distinct epoch of low growth in productivity.

Another bad year was 1974, which stands out as the worst year in all four columns. The drop in average labor productivity in 1974 was so severe that it affects all measures of productivity trends for periods that include 1974. Table 2.3 shows productivity trends as compound annual rates of change during various periods of time. Norsworthy, Harper, and Kunze made their computations from data very similar to those shown in columns 2 and 4 of Table 2.2. Denison's computation is based on data shown in the first column of Table 2.2. These authors calculated trends for different periods of time, but they all show a decline in the growth rate of average labor productivity for the periods that include 1966–1970, and a further decline for the period that includes 1974.

The Importance of 1974

To see how the drop in productivity in 1974 alone affects the computation of trends, suppose we calculate the average year-to-year change in productivity from 1973 through 1978, but simply omit 1974. This can easily be done with the numbers in Table 2.2. Using column 2 of Table 2.2, and basing the average on five years (1973, 1975, 1976, 1977, 1978) instead of six (including 1974), the average is more than 2 percent, instead of the 1.1 percent shown in line 1 of Table 2.3. Doing the same thing with column 4 of Table 2.2, the average is more than 3 percent, instead of the 1.7 percent shown in line 2 of Table 2.3. If it had not been for 1974, the 1973–1978 trend in average labor productivity would have shown no decline from 1965–1973 in the private business sector as a whole, and in manufacturing it would have shown a rebound to the high trend that prevailed from 1948 through 1965.

Figure 2.2 is a picture of ups and downs of labor productivity in manufacturing from 1950 through 1980. The dotted line charts the numbers in column 4 of Table 2.2. The decline in the 1960s is evident, and productivity in 1974 looks as if it fell into a crevasse.

Table 2.3   Average Annual Percentage Rate of Change in Average Labor Productivity or Total Factor Productivity, Selected Studies, Sectors, and Subperiods, 1948–1978

Average Labor Productivity

Norsworthy, Harper, and Kunze

	1948–65	1965–73	1973–78
(1) Private business, total	3.2	2.3	1.1
(2) Manufacturing	3.1	2.4	1.7

Denison

	1948–53	1953–64	1964–69	1969–73	1973–76
(3) Nonresidential business	2.8	2.8	1.8	1.6	−0.5

Total Factor Productivity

Denison

	1948–53	1953–64	1964–69	1969–73	1973–76
(4) Nonresidential business	1.9	2.2	1.8	1.5	−0.9

Kendrick and Grossman

	1948–53	1953–60	1960–66	1966–69	1969–73	1973–76
(5) Private business, total	3.4	2.1	3.4	1.5	1.8	0.7
(6) Manufacturing	2.9	1.1	3.9	0.9	2.7	0.1

Norsworthy, Harper, and Kunze

	1948–65	1965–73	1973–78
(7) Private business, total	2.2	1.2	1.1
(8) Manufacturing	2.5	1.8	1.3

SOURCES: Lines (1), (2), (7), and (8), Norsworthy, Harper, and Kunze, 1979, Tables 2 and 10; lines (3) and (4), Denison, 1979, Tables 2-9 and 4-7; lines (5) and (6), Kendrick and Grossman, 1980, Tables 3-1 and 3-3.

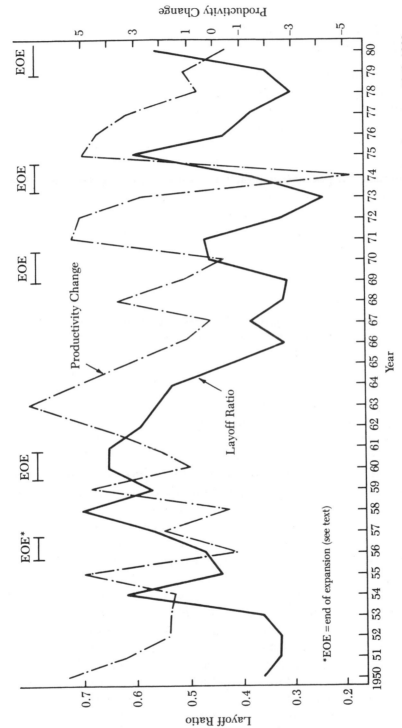

Figure 2.2 Layoff Ratio and Year-to-Year Percentage Change in Average Labor Productivity, U.S. Manufacturing, 1950–1980.

Growth-Accounting and Measurement of Total Factor Productivity

The most thorough attempts to explain changes in productivity in the United States have used the growth-accounting procedures developed by Edward Denison and John Kendrick. These procedures are designed to measure how much of the growth in real output over time can be attributed to growth in the amounts of labor and capital employed. Capital includes inventories, structures, and equipment. Generally, output and capital have grown faster than labor. For example, Denison's data show that real output in the nonresidential business sector just about doubled between 1950 and 1971, as did the constant-dollar value of nonresidential business capital (Denison, 1979, Tables 2-6 and 4-1). But total employment in nonresidential business grew less than 25 percent in that time (Denison, Table 2-7). The task of growth-accounting is to decide how much of the growth in output is attributable to growth in labor or capital. For example, since both output and capital approximately doubled between 1950 and 1971, it might be tempting to conclude simply that all the growth in output is attributable to growth in capital. But then how to explain recessions, when the capital stock usually keeps growing even though employment and output decline? At such times it appears that employment is the limiting factor.

In practice, growth-accounting does not assume that capital is responsible for growth at some times and labor at other times. Instead, the growth rates of labor and capital are combined into a growth rate for total factor input. The procedure is to multiply the growth rate of labor by the proportion of total output that is paid to labor in wages, salaries, and other compensation. The resulting number is called labor's contribution to growth of output. Similarly, capital's contribution to growth of output is the growth rate of capital multiplied by the share of total output that is paid for use of capital. The rationale for computing the contributions of labor and capital in this way is that the amount of output paid to either factor of production reflects both the physical amount of that factor being used and the payment for each physical unit employed. The payment per physical unit is assumed to reflect the amount of output that would be produced if one more physical unit were employed. Specifically, the ratio of money paid for a unit of labor to money paid for use of a unit of capital equals the ratio of additional output from a unit of labor to additional output from a unit of capital. No one claims that this assumption is true all the time; some say it is hardly ever true.

However realistic or unrealistic this assumption may be, it permits the computation to be made: A 10 percent increase in the capital stock would contribute about 2 percent to growth of output, because about one fifth of total output is paid for use of capital. A 10 percent increase in employment would contribute about 8 percent to growth of output, because about four fifths of total output is paid for labor.

The assumption that payments to productive factors reflect differences in the productive value of those factors also determines how growth-accounting defines "quality of labor." Females generally are paid less than males, so they are assumed to be that much less productive. Younger workers are paid less than older ones. Employees with more education on average are paid more than employees with less education. Standard procedure in growth-accounting is to use observed differences in earnings between groups to make an index of labor quality. In effect, young or female employees are assumed to contribute less. This assumption is incorrect to the extent that lower earnings for these groups result from discrimination or historical custom. Less arbitrary measures of the productive capacity of the work force could be constructed from data on the actual productivity of a representative cross-section of individuals in different kinds of jobs—but such data do not exist.*

Once the indexes of effective labor and capital input have been constructed, the contributions of each input to growth in output can be computed. The sum of the contributions of capital and labor is called the contribution of total factor input to growth in output. Curiously enough, the actual growth of output is usually more than the contribution of total factor input. "Total factor productivity" is the difference.

For example, according to Denison, real output of nonresidential business grew at a compound annual rate of 3.56 percent from 1948

---

* Martin Baily cites some rather bizarre evidence on earnings differences and sex in his comments on the paper by Norsworthy, Harper, and Kunze. This evidence implies that differences in earnings do *not* reflect differences in productivity. It "comes from a follow-up survey of persons who had actually changed sex. One hundred seventy follow-up interviews were conducted by a Stanford psychiatrist. *The New York Times* of October 2, 1979, reports that all those changing from female to male earned more after the change. Most of those changing from male to female earned less. Three males who changed to females decided to resume living as males. Two of the three cited inability to do well economically as the reason. The third had a religious experience." Baily is sure no one will take this evidence seriously, however.

to 1973. The labor index contributed 1.02 percent to this annual growth rate, and the capital index contributed 0.56 percent, so "total factor input" contributed the sum of these, or 1.58 percent. The difference between the actual growth rate of output and the contribution of total factor input is 3.56 minus 1.58, or 1.98 percent. This is the annual growth rate of total factor productivity, which Denison calls "output per unit of input" (Denison, 1979, Table 7-1). In other words, most of the 3.56 percent-a-year growth in output from 1948 to 1973 is *not attributed to growth in employment and capital*. It is attributed to some set of "residual" factors, which are presumed to cause growth in total factor productivity.

The Mysterious Drop in Total Factor Productivity

The fact that much of the growth in output is not attributed to growth in capital and labor inputs has long been an intellectual puzzle for economists. As long as growth in residual factors is stable or increasing, the problem has no practical urgency. But now it appears that growth in total factor productivity, like average labor productivity, has diminished. Lines 4 through 8 in Table 2.3 present various estimates of the annual growth rate of total factor productivity. All show a reduction after the mid-1960s, and another drop after 1973.

Table 2.3 shows some difference in the estimates of how much of the slowdown occurred before and after 1973. Kendrick and Grossman show one distinct slowdown in 1966–1969, a partial recovery in 1969–1973, and an even more abrupt slowdown in 1973–1976. Denison shows trends for slightly different periods. His 1964–1969 period begins with a couple of years of rapid growth in productivity, which may be the reason why this period looks better than Kendrick and Grossman's 1966–1969 period, relative to the years before and after. Denison does find a steep drop in the growth rate of total factor productivity after 1973, as do Kendrick and Grossman. But Norsworthy, Harper, and Kunze show a more gradual drop after 1973.

In his written comments on their paper, Denison offered an explanation for the difference between his results and those of Norsworthy, Harper, and Kunze. He asserted, "The reason for this difference is my inclusion of an estimate for the effect of fluctuations in intensity of demand . . . ." Denison estimated how much difference this would make in their computed rates of growth of total factor productivity in the private business sector as a whole for 1948–1965, 1965–1973, and 1973–1978. Instead of 2.2, 1.2, and 1.1 percent, respectively, Denison's adjustment for "intensity of demand" would yield growth rates of 2.1, 1.9, and 1.1 percent. This adjustment therefore makes the results of Norsworthy, Harper, and Kunze more similar to Denison's own, and also more similar to those of Kendrick and Grossman: some decline in growth of total factor productivity in the late 1960s, and an even sharper decline after 1973.

Denison's Accounting for Trends in Total Factor Productivity

The adjustment for fluctuations in intensity of demand is part of the procedure Denison developed to account for growth in total factor productivity. He also measures other variables thought to explain why output can grow at a different rate than the total input of capital and labor. These other variables are:

- Improved resource allocation due to labor moving from farming and self-employment to more productive activity;
- Laws and regulations requiring pollution abatement and better protection of workers' safety and health;
- Dishonesty and crime among employees;
- Economies of scale;
- Weather;
- Labor disputes;
- Change in number of work days from year to year (e.g., due to leap years).

Finally, Denison leaves an irreducible residual category—advances in knowledge and n.e.c. (not elsewhere classified)—to include the influences of unmeasured factors.

In his 1979 book, Denison concluded that the decline in growth of total factor productivity (output per unit of input) could be attributed to the influence of measured variables—including intensity of demand—up to 1973, but not after. That is, the decline in growth of output per unit of input up to 1973 does not require explanation in terms of unmeasured variables. But after 1973 changes in the measured variables listed above do *not* account for the estimated decline in growth of output per unit of input. In fact, the *whole* reduction in growth of total factor productivity, shown here on line 4 of Table 2.3, must be attributed to unmeasured variables. These influences appear to have had an absolute negative effect on output after 1973— they made output shrink, not grow. This result raises doubts about whether these residual influences should be called "advances in knowledge." As Denison put it, apart from "calamities like the fall of the Roman Empire," advances in knowledge can only have a positive effect on productivity. The apparent negative effect was "the dominant development of the period" (pp. 80–81).

Denison acknowledged, "What happened is, to be blunt, a mystery" (p. 4). He examined 17 different suspects, some measurable and some not. He found cause for a lot more research, but not for an indictment. The 17 are:

- Curtailment of expenditures on research and development;
- Decline in opportunity for major new advances;
- Decline of Yankee ingenuity and deterioration of American technology;
- Increased lag in the application of knowledge due to the aging of capital;
- Diversion of input to comply with government regulation, except pollution and safety (which Denison already accounted for);
- Government-imposed paperwork;
- Regulation and taxation: diversion of executive attention;
- Government regulation: delay of new projects;
- Regulation and taxation: misallocation of resources;
- Effects of high tax rates on incentives and efficiency;
- Capital gains provisions of the Revenue Act of 1969;
- "People don't want to work any more";
- Impairment of efficiency by inflation;
- Lessening of competitive pressure and changes in the quality of management;
- The rise in energy prices;
- The shift to services and other structural changes; and
- Possible errors in the data.

Denison reviewed each of these arguments, rejected some, and characterized others as "probably correct, but, individually, able to explain only a small part of the slowdown" (p. 4). Who or what killed productivity growth is still a very open question.

Kendrick and Grossman's Analysis

Kendrick and Grossman tried to shed some light on the question by analyzing differences in productivity growth among 20 manufacturing industries. First they identified characteristics of industries where total factor productivity grew faster than in other industries from 1948 to 1966. These included such things as the percentage of workers belonging to unions and expenditures on research and development. Then they looked at whether these same characteristics were also present in industries where productivity grew faster than in other industries from 1966 to 1976. If the characteristics of industries with fast-growing productivity were the same in the two periods, Kendrick and Grossman would have concluded that the general decline in productivity growth was attributable to changes in the average prevalence of these characteristics. However, they found instead that "the underlying factors of productivity gains—as identified here—are unstable" (p. 111). The mystery persists.

A Clue

"The finding that the unexplained slowdown in productivity growth started only after 1973 . . . is an important clue," according to Denison (p. 145). Several of the 17 suspects he examined can be exonerated for the simple reason that their behavior did not change suddenly in 1973. Energy prices are an exception, but Denison concluded that the sudden rise in energy prices could explain only a very small fraction of the decrease in productivity. Is there anything else that did change suddenly in 1973?

The Layoff Ratio and the Job Security Effect

Figure 2.2 shows the history of two quantities from 1950 to 1980. One, the year-to-year change in average labor productivity in manufacturing, shows an unprecedented drop in 1974. The other shows an unprecedented drop in 1973. This other quantity is the layoff rate in manufacturing, divided by the sum of the quit rate and the layoff rate in manufacturing. I will call this the "layoff ratio" for short. A layoff is a permanent or temporary separation for which the employer is considered responsible. A quit is a separation for which the employee is considered responsible. Changes in the layoff ratio reflect changes in the proportion of separations for which employers are responsible. Data on quits and layoffs are collected in the United States from manufacturing establishments, but not from other major sectors of the economy. That is why Figure 2.2 refers only to manufacturing.

The correspondence between the unprecedented 1974 drop in growth of average labor productivity and the unprecedented drop in the layoff ratio in 1973 is not the only feature these two series have in common. In fact, almost every turning point in the layoff ratio is soon followed by a turning point in productivity growth. Specifically, the corresponding dates are:

	Layoff Ratio	*Productivity Growth*
Trough	1951–1952	1952–1954
Peak	1954	1955
Trough	1955	1956
Peak	1958	1959
Trough	1959	1960
Peak	1960–1961	1963
Trough	1966	1967
Peak	1967	1968
Trough	1969	1970
Peak	1970–1971	1971–1972
Trough	1973	1974
Peak	1975	1975
Trough	1978	

The fact that two quantities appear to move together over time in no way proves that one causes the other. But there is reason to believe that conditions reflected by the layoff ratio do have a causal effect on average productivity of labor. A rise in the layoff ratio means a larger proportion of job separations are being decided by employers. There is less job security for employees. A fall in the layoff ratio means a larger proportion of job separations are occurring because employees are choosing to quit. More choices are open to employees. The layoff ratio is therefore a measure of the bargaining power of employers relative to employees. When employers have more power, they are in a position to demand more or better work from employees. If employees do not comply, they can be replaced more easily at times when many laid-off people are looking for work. So when the layoff ratio is high or has risen recently, employees tend to become more willing to do what supervisors request or command, including work that was formerly the responsibility of other employees just laid off. Conversely, if the layoff ratio is low or falling, employees who feel their supervisors' demands are excessive are in a better position to quit.

This is not a new theory. Wesley C. Mitchell, a contemporary of John Dewey, observed that

> *in the later stages of expansion . . . the maintenance of shop discipline becomes difficult—the penalty of discharge is less dreaded when jobs are easy to get.* (quoted in Oster, p. 339)

Similarly, John Kendrick, a leading contemporary business economist much in the tradition of Mitchell, has written that

> *. . . the degree of labor efficiency, relative to realizable standards or "norms," affects productivity. Changes in efficiency, so defined, as revealed by "work measurement," should seem largely to depend on motivational factors, given the institutional framework. Labor efficiency, like utilization rates, seems to have a systematic cyclical component. That is, productivity rises before the trough, as the profit squeeze increases managements' cost consciousness, and as* rising unemployment motivates workers to value their jobs more highly and work more productively. *The reverse of these factors may help account for the slowdown of productivity gains before cycle peaks.* (Kendrick, 1976, p. 5; emphasis added.)

Influence of the Overhead Labor Effect

Although the likely negative effect of job security on employees' motivation and productivity has long been acknowledged, it has never been included in standard quantitative models of the business cycle. One reason is that the influence of job security is smaller than another effect, sometimes called the "overhead labor effect." The overhead labor effect and the job security effect work in opposite directions.

The overhead labor effect occurs because changes in employment tend to lag behind changes in output. When sales and output decline due to an unexpected fall in demand, employers do not reduce employment as fast as output. It may just take time for an employer to realize that business has fallen off—in a retail operation, for example, management may review total sales figures only weekly or monthly. The employer may also want to make sure the decline in business is not just temporary. Also, economists have increasingly realized the importance of "implicit contracts" between employers and employees, establishing long-term employment relationships in which employees have some protection against layoffs when business fluctuates. (See Okun, 1981; Hall, 1980.) For reasons such as these, some employees are kept on the payroll even when there is less work for them to do. This is "overhead labor." The effect is that average labor productivity declines when output does.

Eventually, when the fall in business is seen to be more than temporary, layoffs ensue. Then, when business begins to recover, laid-off workers are recalled or new people are hired. But again there is a lag. It takes time for managers to obtain the sales data and to decide that an increase in employment is warranted. Hiring new people may entail an investment in training as new employment relationships are created. So output grows faster than employment. The overhead labor effect operates in reverse: as output increases, so does average labor productivity.

The fact that output and average labor productivity usually change in the same direction, due to the overhead labor effect, has been documented in dozens, perhaps hundreds, of studies (see Okun, 1981). It is the basis for procedures, like Denison's adjustment for intensity of demand, that are designed to separate the short-term, cyclical component of productivity change from any change in long-term trend (Denison, 1979, Appendix I).

Gordon's "End-of-Expansion Phenomenon"

Recently, however, the puzzling results obtained by Denison and others have stimulated efforts to refine the standard quantitative models of short-run changes in productivity. For example, Robert J. Gordon has estimated a model which, in addition to the usual overhead labor effect, also demonstrates the "often overlooked but consistent tendency for productivity to perform poorly in the last stages of a business expansion" (p. 448). The periods during which Gordon estimates this tendency to have occurred are shown in Figure 2.2 by the horizontal lines labelled EOE. These certainly are periods of diminished growth in productivity. Gordon concluded that taking the end-of-expansion phenomenon into account can improve economic forecasting, though he found no ready explanation for the phenomenon itself.

Other studies have found evidence that the end-of-expansion phenomenon may be at least partly explained by the job security effect. Robert J. Gordon did not consider the job security effect as a possible explanation, but studies by David M. Gordon, by Stern and Friedman, and by Gerry Oster all found evidence that the job security effect partially offsets the overhead labor effect.

Combined Effects of Job Security and Overhead Labor

Over the business cycle, the two effects would operate as follows. The expansion begins with output rising faster than employment, so average labor productivity is rising. As the layoff ratio falls and employees relax a bit, productivity growth diminishes. The job security effect is not the only reason for diminishing productivity growth at this point; shortages of materials and use of back-up equipment also contribute to this end-of-expansion decline. If demand is still growing, employers will keep increasing output, but to do so they will have to increase employment at an even faster rate. More hiring and lower productivity growth feed on each other, as employers increase overtime and put more people on the payroll to meet production targets, and the consequent tightening of labor markets makes employees less afraid of supervisors. Eventually productivity may decline absolutely. Meanwhile, costs have been rising. If rising costs are not passed on in rising prices, profits are squeezed, and this slows the expansion of business. If rising costs do get passed on in rising prices, the government eventually has to use its monetary and fiscal policies to slow inflation, which also has the result of slowing the expansion. If total demand actually declines, employment at first will not decline as fast, so productivity falls further. Then the layoff ratio rises, usually rather abruptly. Productivity rises as employment falls faster than output, in what could be called the end-of-contraction phenomenon. Job insecurity contributes to this rise in productivity, as does the shutting down of relatively unproductive equipment and facilities. When the next recovery begins, those employees who remain on the payroll are relatively willing to put out the extra effort to handle the new increase in business.

Empirical Evidence of the Job Security Effect

This schematic description of a business cycle is consistent with the quantitative descriptions of the "average" business cycle, as constructed by Kendrick and Grossman. The role of the job security effect in this account is also consistent with the two lines in Figure

2.2 and with the other studies cited. Some economists, however, are inclined to be skeptical of the job security effect. For example, Alan Blinder, commenting about the productivity puzzle of the 1970s, wrote:

> *The most obvious cause of a drop in productivity would be if a given worker, working under unchanged conditions, became less efficient or less hard working. While this anthropomorphic interpretation of the word "productivity" probably best captures the layman's understanding of the word, it has precious little to do with the actual performance of measured productivity.* (Blinder, 1979, p. 64)

Blinder's use of the word "anthropomorphic" is strange, since employees are in fact human. But his point is that the overhead labor effect can explain most of the variation in productivity.

If all we had was the kind of evidence shown in Figure 2.2, we could not distinguish between the overhead labor effect and the job security effect. Changes in the layoff ratio precede changes in productivity growth. This is consistent with the job security effect. But since a rise in layoffs is caused by a business contraction, Figure 2.2 could be interpreted to mean nothing more than that a rise in layoffs during a contraction tends to be followed by a rise in productivity as the next recovery begins. Making causal inferences from correlated time series is tricky.

Of the studies to date that have demonstrated the job security effect, the one that most successfully overcomes this ambiguity is Gerry Oster's. Oster uses the overall unemployment rate as the measure of job insecurity (the unemployment rate and layoff ratio are highly correlated over time), and finds it to be positively associated with changes in productivity in every major U.S. manufacturing industry taken separately. The job security effect evidently does operate apart from the overhead labor effect. Furthermore, a high rate of unemployment in the economy as a whole is estimated to stimulate productivity most in industries where smaller proportions of employees belong to unions and where smaller proportions of employees receive any specific training in their jobs. These results are what one would expect, since union contracts usually regulate layoffs and reduce the uncertainty on which the productivity-enhancing effect of layoffs or unemployment depends. And since specific training of an employee usually requires some investment by the employer (for example, instruction given on company time), employees who have received specific training can expect more stable employment. Oster's results make sense.

The Job Security Effect and Growth-Accounting

The job security effect has implications for growth-accounting. If Denison had included an adjustment for the job security effect, which would account for some of the drop in productivity in 1974, he could have made the period after 1973 much less mysterious. It is possible that this adjustment would also make some other period look more mysterious. And there are other theories that have been proposed to solve Denison's mystery without any reference to the job security effect. In particular, Martin Baily has suggested that the rise in oil prices in 1973 had the effect of making energy-wasting equipment and buildings obsolete. This would also help explain why the market value of corporate stock has been less than the book value of capital assets (Baily, 1981). Unfortunately, it is generally difficult to obtain separate empirical estimates of change in the productivity of capital or labor by themselves. The years 1973–1974 are especially difficult to explain because they encompassed several unusual events in addition to the dip in the layoff ratio: the rise in oil prices, the Watergate investigation, and the resignation of President Nixon.

Whether the job security effect will ultimately advance the practice of growth-accounting remains to be seen.

The Job Security Effect and Economic Policy

Recognition of the job security effect as a factor in business cycles has definite implications for economic policy. If increasing job security tends to reduce productivity growth, then policies designed to achieve full employment will tend to be self-defeating because reducing growth in productivity will aggravate inflation. Given the job security effect, attempting to sustain full employment will cause inflation to accelerate, as others have argued for different reasons.

But the job security effect is not necessarily a given. Work in contemporary organizations is often more than just a way to make a living. In a long-lasting employment relationship, gains for both employer and employee may be greatest when motivational strategies emphasize the positive value of work well done, rather than the threat of termination. Some of the value of work well done may be measured in money, some in the intrinsic satisfaction of effective performance. To the extent that these positive motivations come into play, the threat of termination is irrelevant. If the threat of termination diminishes in relevance to day-to-day work, the job security effect should diminish. If the threat had no force at all, the job security effect on productivity would not exist.

Whether in fact the job security effect can ever be entirely eliminated, and whether that would also eliminate end-of-expansion declines in productivity growth, so that economic expansions and high employment could be more prolonged, no one knows. But making the threat of termination less relevant to motivation in more jobs, by emphasizing the positive value of effective performance, should weaken the job security effect and help prolong high employment. The following sections explain how this can be, and in some companies has been, done. On the strength of these actual examples and others like them, this chapter will end with some definite conclusions about national economic policy.

Productivity and Motivation

Various motivational strategies for productive organizations have been described by psychologists. According to one account, contemporary psychology views "the performance of a person on a job . . . as a function of two different kinds of variables. One of these refers to the ability or skill of the individual to perform the job and the second refers to his motivation to use this ability or skill in the actual performance of the job" (Vroom and Deci, 1970, p. 10). It is possible to identify at least three distinct managerial or organizational strategies for stimulating motivation. Vroom and Deci label one approach "paternalistic": "The essence of this approach is to make the organization a source of important rewards—rewards for which the only qualification is membership in the organization" (p. 11). An all-important sanction wielded by paternalistic management is termination of an employee's membership in the organization: Be a dutiful worker or be fired.

A second approach is based on the "scientific management" methods first developed by Frederick W. Taylor. The key assumption is that "a person will be motivated to work if rewards and penalties are tied directly to his performance," (p. 13) rather than accruing automatically as a perquisite of employment. Where company pension plans and picnics are typical rewards offered by paternalistic management, scientific management relies instead on piece rates and bonus pay. For employees who fail to meet minimum standards, however, the threat of firing still applies.

A third approach, of more recent origin, is called "participative management" by Vroom and Deci:

> *Whereas paternalistic management assumed that man can be induced to work out of a feeling of gratitude to the system, and the external control system associated with scientific management assumed that man can be induced to work by the expectation of gain for doing or the expectation of loss for not doing, participative management assumes that individuals can derive satisfaction from doing an effective job per se. They can become ego-involved in their jobs, emotionally committed to doing them well and take pride from evidence that they are effective in furthering the objectives of the company.* (p. 15)

This strategy emphasizes intrinsic motivation rather than extrinsic rewards:

> *Incentives for effective performance are in the task or job itself or in the individual's relationship with members of his working team, not in the organizationally mediated consequences of task performance. The emphasis is on creating conditions under which effective performance can be a goal rather than a means to the attainment of some other goal, and the philosophy is one of self-control or self-regulation rather than organizational control.* (p. 16)

Redesigning Jobs for Intrinsic Motivation: Experience of the Late 1960s and Early 1970s

In the late 1960s and early 1970s there was a great deal of interest, both in the United States and abroad, in how to make work more intrinsically motivating. Many companies tried out "job enrichment" or other kinds of "job redesign," sometimes as part of larger efforts to improve the "quality of working life" (see Chapter 3). Accounts of these efforts, published in the early 1970s, were often enthusiastic. Some saw the possibility of a whole new economic order based on intrinsically motivating, rather than alienating, work (Jenkins, 1973; Sheppard and Herrick, 1972; O'Toole, 1973). Others saw intrinsic motivation as a humane but basically practical way to increase workers' productivity (Rush, 1971; Maher, 1971; Herzberg, 1968; Greenblatt, 1973; Kraft and Williams, 1975; Paul, Robertson, and Herzberg, 1969).

What constitutes an effective intrinsic-motivation strategy depends on the personalities and cultures of the employees involved, and on the climate and structure of the employing organization. The complexity and subtlety of these variables themselves make intrinsic-motivation strategies difficult to design and implement. More will be said in the next chapter about the obstacles to intrinsic-motivation strategies. In spite of the complexities, some general principles did emerge from experience through the early 1970s. In a report for the National Science Foundation in January 1975, Katzell, Yankelovich, and associates summarized some of what could be learned from published case reports and field research:

> *The key ingredients of a generally motivating job, as suggested by the*
> *. . . data, include:*
> a. *sufficient difficulty to be challenging;*
> b. *sufficient diversity to be interesting;*
> c. *constructive interaction with others;*
> d. *a work cycle sufficiently long that the work is not repetitive or*
>   *monotonous;*
> e. *sufficient identity or wholeness of the task to represent a meaning-*
>   *ful share of the product or service;*
> f. *regular and frequent feedback concerning the consequences of one's*
>   *work;*
> g. *considerable self-control over one's work;*
> h. *direct responsibility for the welfare of others outside one's im-*
>   *mediate work group, especially customers or clients—a concept*
>   *sometimes termed "stewardship."* (pp. 184–185)

But by the time this was published, the rush to "job enrichment" and other intrinsic-motivation strategies appeared to be losing momentum. Richard Hackman, one of the leaders in research on design of motivating jobs, warned of the "Coming Demise of Job Enrichment" (1975). The fad petered out not because the theory of intrinsic motivation was suddenly disproven, just as it did not begin because of any startling new psychological discovery (Katzell and Yankelovich, 1975; Strauss, 1974). The surge of interest in techniques for improving intrinsic motivation occurred in the United States at a time when unemployment rates were very low, from 1965 to 1970. Although this period was also unusual in other ways, one reason why employers became especially interested in ideas such as participative management and job enrichment at this time appears to have been that more traditional approaches to motivating workers were less effective in such a tight labor market. When employees know that jobs are plentiful, the threat of firing becomes less effective in producing compliance with employers' demands. To offset the negative effect on job attachment and productivity, managers had to seek other techniques for motivating workers. Similarly, when unemployment rates rose again in the 1970s, the threat of firing regained its former potency, and this could explain why managers became less concerned with employees' intrinsic motivation.

Reversion to Traditional Strategies for Motivation in the 1970s

The frequency with which employees quit their jobs is one indication of how unmanageable the work force is. The quit rate in manufacturing averaged less than 1.5 percent a month from 1960 to 1965, then rose to more than 2.5 percent a month from 1966 through 1969, as unemployment was kept under 4 percent. In 1970, when unemployment rose sharply, the quit rate quickly dropped back below 2 percent (U.S. Department of Labor, 1976). A statistical study of quit rates from 1951 to 1970 by the Bureau of Labor Statistics concluded, "Workers are very conscious of job security and can have their confidence shaken very easily . . ." (U.S. Department of Labor, 1973, p. 28).

Statements by managers suggest that the rise in unemployment rates in the early 1970s may have had an especially sobering effect on younger workers who had built up little or no entitlement to unemployment insurance, and whose prior attitudes may have been most antiauthoritarian. As one vice-president of employee relations put it in 1976, the recession of 1974–1975 "could be a blessing in disguise. . . . I think young people in the next few years will take a different attitude in terms of appreciating the job they have." Another top executive agreed, "Young workers have gotten the '60s out of their system, and they've got their feet on the ground more than the teenagers of a few years ago" (Hoerr, 1976).

It appears that there may be a tendency for employers to revert to paternalistic or extrinsic-motivation strategies when unemployment rates are high and the threat of firing is taken seriously by employees. When unemployment rates are low, employers apparently become more willing to try intrinsic-motivation strategies. Further evidence that the tightness of labor markets generally affects employers' choice of management strategies is presented in the next chapter. At this point it is useful to have a couple of examples from specific companies.

Providing for Intrinsic Motivation:
The Example of AT&T

Important examples of "motivation through the work itself" were provided by Robert N. Ford and his associates at American Telephone and Telegraph Company in the late 1960s. These examples are important because AT&T has some of the characteristics of both a large, private corporation and a government agency. What has been learned at AT&T, therefore, has implications for both the public and private sectors. The reforms at AT&T in the 1960s are also important as examples of humanistic psychology—in the tradition of Abraham Maslow, Douglas McGregor, Frederick Herzberg, Rensis Likert, and others. Ford's widely cited book is dedicated "to Professor Frederick Herzberg, humanist and psychologist." Herzberg's "two-factor" theory—that improving material conditions and extrinsic rewards may reduce or prevent employees' *dis*satisfaction, but positive satisfaction in a job comes only from intrinsic interest in the work itself—provided a rationale for trying to design jobs for the people in them. This was a fairly new idea at the time, and still cannot be said to represent standard managerial practice.

What AT&T Did

Another important feature of the reforms at AT&T in the late 1960s is the clarity of the company's own motivation. Ford's book begins, "The problem that precipitated the studies in this book is employee turnover." After presenting some data on rising turnover, Ford observed,

> *Unemployment hit a 15-year low in November of 1968 . . . . Obviously, there is a connection between the high employee turnover rate and a low national unemployment rate. When jobs are plentiful, a person does not have to keep an undesirable job; he simply leaves.* (pp. 13–14)

The job security effect—indicated by low unemployment rates, or a low layoff ratio in Figure 2.2—had become acute. This is what made top management at AT&T receptive to trying the new motivational strategies Ford and his group were proposing. The fact that "job security is virtually unsurpassed" (p. 15) in the Bell system (except by college teaching and some public employment) also helps to explain why AT&T has continued to develop intrinsic-motivation strategies even after the rise in national unemployment made the problem of recruiting and retaining productive employees less acute.

The original trial took place in New York City from March to September 1965. It involved 104 young women whose job was to answer letters and another 16 who answered telephone inquiries— whether from shareholders or customers (or customers who were also shareholders) is ambiguous from Ford's account (pp. 21, 26). Seventy percent of the "girls" were college graduates. The third-level and fourth-level supervisors agreed with the project director on a list of seven changes, which one of the third-level supervisors then proposed to the second-level supervisor who transmitted them to the first-level supervisor in charge of the experimental group of 20 letter writers.

The seven changes were described by Ford:

1. *Subject matter experts were appointed within each unit for other members of the unit to consult with before seeking supervisor help. (Later on, it was found that the girls had rearranged these assignments among themselves along lines they felt to be more meaningful. This was a real test of the climate of responsibility we were trying to build, and it was accepted as such by management.)*
2. *Correspondents were told to sign their own names to letters from the very first day on the job after training. (They were simple letters, to be sure, but previously the verifier or supervisor usually signed for many months.)*
3. *The work of the more experienced correspondents was looked over less frequently by supervisors, and this was done at each correspondent's desk. Verification dropped from 100 percent to 10 percent. (This can be a source of significant dollar savings—$12,000 per group per year, if quality holds up, or more if it improves.)*
4. *Production was discussed, but only in general terms: "A full day's work is expected," for example. (As time went on, the supervisors said, it was not necessary even to mention production. Less pressure than usual is the direction of this change.)*
5. *Outgoing work went directly to the mailroom without crossing the supervisor's desk. (Oddly enough, some experienced workers had trouble in breaking up this dependent relationship.)*
6. *All correspondents were told they would be held fully accountable for quality of work. (Prior to that, responsibility was shared with verifiers and supervisors.)*
7. *Correspondents were encouraged to answer letters in a more personalized way, avoiding the previous form-letter approach. (If a customer's letter is complicated, this can actually lead to better service and a higher quality index.)* (pp. 29–30)

These changes were introduced at the rate of about one a week.

First-level supervisors in the experimental and other groups were kept uninformed about the experiment, as were the girls themselves. The intent was to avoid a Hawthorne effect.

Results were very promising. Members of the experimental group showed a definite increase in positive answers to questionnaire items like, "How many opportunities do you feel you have in your job for making worthwhile contributions?" They gave more negative answers to questions like, "How often have you felt unable to use your full capabilities in the performance of your job?" Other groups showed no change or a slight worsening of expressed attitudes during the study period. The changes apparently did have a psychological impact, and there also appeared to be a payoff in reduced turnover. Ford reported that only one girl resigned from the experimental group, because she disliked the added responsibility. Turnover in the other groups continued at the former "high" levels (pp. 26, 35). Findings on turnover were clouded, however, by "some natural shrinkage," from 120 to 95 girls in the whole study, over the six months (p. 27). Ford's original account for AT&T does not tell how the departure of one out of every four employees in the original study group was distributed among the experimental and other units, or how it affected attitudes.

But plenty of Bell managers saw sufficient promise in the original study that they requested replication and improvement of job design in parts of the organization for which they were responsible. Ford's book reports that the results elsewhere in the department where the original study took place "are impressive. The results in the eight service representative trials are quite large; this is the best single sample." Gains in other departments were described as "visible and consistent" or "modest." One department reported "no difference," but in no trial did the experimental group do worse than the control group (p. 78). The bottom line:

> *The most striking single piece of evidence was a 13 percent drop in the [annual] turnover rate among a large sample of service representatives at a time when the control group rate increased by 9 percent. Other technical results (productivity, quality of performance, customer reaction, and so on) either improved slightly or at least held their own. If the turnover rate across the Bell system could be dropped by only 10 percentage points (to use a conservative figure), the savings in training costs on this one job alone would be in millions of dollars.* (pp. 188–189)

That does not include possible savings from enabling supervisors to take charge of more people.

Some of the flavor of the situation at AT&T in 1965–1967 and the effect of these trials is best conveyed by first-hand accounts. Fred Foulkes, a sympathetic observer of the AT&T trials, describes one office that was "short eight people, and turnover was very high." At a meeting with his four supervisors, the manager "focused on the best way to develop the new employees. He said it was clear that a supervisor would have to spend more time with the new people and less with the experienced people." One supervisor "suggested that girls be made responsible for checking their own vouchers . . . . The manager adopted the idea of 'time savers for supervisors,' and additional . . . items were discussed at each weekly supervisory meeting" (pp. 142–143).

In another story told to Foulkes by a division manager, "a supervisor had delegated the responsibility of training a new worker to one of her girls. The girl was elated by this opportunity, which not only gave her recognition but permitted the supervisor to see what kind of talent she really had" (p. 139). Foulkes gave another example of positive results noted approvingly by high-level management. Shortly after the original study in the letter-writing office,

> *a transportation strike severely crippled the city . . . . While the overall absenteeism rate was extremely high on the first day of the strike, the attendance of the achieving [i.e., experimental] group was perfect. One executive said these girls felt they had an important job to do, and they found a way to get to work so they could do it. Many employees did not report for work until the fourth day of the transportation strike, but the attendance of the achieving group was perfect throughout.*

The studies at AT&T in 1965–1967 produced numerical results that made "job improvement" appear virtually free of downside risk. It wouldn't *hurt*. And high-level managers were saying good things about it. Middle management had every incentive to buy in. Ford and his associates continued to promote the idea. By 1973, there was evidence that these efforts had had a widespread effect on turnover at AT&T. Peter Henle, an economist at the U.S. Bureau of Labor Statistics, wrote about the difficulty of measuring economic effects of any changes in employees' attitudes, using published or unpublished government data. Quit rates were a possible indicator, but in manufacturing and mining there were no clear trends or patterns. However, in the communications sector,

> *Although there was a slow but steady increase in the quit rate during the 1960s, a sharp drop beginning in 1969 left the 1972 rate at a new*

*record low. According to industry officials, the drop can be attributed
to at least two factors: a higher wage schedule for low-skill jobs, and a
program of job enrichment initiated by the Bell system.* (p. 126)

We cannot be sure to what extent the drop in 1969 was caused by
the spreading of Ford's program, although his book did come out
that year.

As of 1981, the program of "motivation through the work itself" at
AT&T appeared to have evolved into a "quality of work life" effort,
with the Communication Workers of America participating. The
written agreement included this statement: "Management and
union seek to better acknowledge, employ, and develop the potential of all employees and are committed to providing the necessary
information and training . . ." (*World of Work Report*, August 1981,
p. 64).

Discussion of the AT&T Case

Robert Ford described an analogy he sometimes used to explain the
idea of work itself as a motivating force to people who were slow to
understand. He likened the "well-motivated employee" to a serious
recreational golfer. "Neither goes around grinning happily all the
time." But both are interested in what they are doing because it
offers the chance for achievement, recognition, and growth. For the
golfer, as for the employee, "the *responsibility* is all his" (p. 93).

This analogy conveys some of the spirit of Ford's own work, and
some of the limitations of his theory. For one thing, golf is a particularly individualistic activity. One's score does not depend directly on
other players. Some paid work is also solitary, but in most jobs it is
impossible to get the work done without the collaboration of other
people. Ford's principles of intrinsic motivation are based on individual responses; it is not clear how they apply to groups.

A more obvious limitation implied by Ford's analogy is the lack of
attention to questions of equity. A recreational golfer does not get
paid to play, but employees do get paid to work, because what they
produce is presumably wanted by someone else. But workers who
are not self-employed do not sell the product or service themselves.
The employer does, and the employer tries to make a profit, unless
it is a government agency or nonprofit organization. Between the
employee and the employer, there is always some division of revenues from sales. What constitutes an equitable division is, to say the
least, a pervasive issue. It is a question that arises when employees

are invited to participate in any work-restructuring that gives them more responsibility.

The psychological humanists have been attacked on this point by trade unionists and others. Mitchell Fein, for example, has been a persistent critic of the purely psychological approach to redesigning jobs. He insists that what motivates people to produce is monetary reward. Without that, "workers perceive it as the boss getting something for nothing" (*Training* magazine, March 1981, p. 28).

Some programs for improving productivity face up squarely to this issue by giving employees a "piece of the action"—sharing cash bonuses when productivity improves. Fein promotes one such program, called Improshare. An older approach is the well-known Scanlon plan. The usually hard-nosed General Accounting Office of Congress has reported that such programs can in fact increase average productivity (*World of Work Report*, August 1981, p. 64).

The Scanlon Plan

The Scanlon plan originated in the 1930s when Joseph Scanlon, then a union officer in a Pennsylvania steel mill, devised an agreement between the union and management that brought the company through financial crisis by enlisting workers to improve efficiency. Increased wages ensued. Scanlon moved to union headquarters, then went to work at MIT with Douglas McGregor. Here the plan was formulated and refined through experience in a number of companies (Katzell and Yankelovich 1975, pp. 355–356).

There appears to have been a revival of interest in the Scanlon plan in American industry in the late 1960s and early 1970s when so many managers were looking for new motivational strategies. A report in 1977 estimated that "more than 100" Scanlon plans were then in operation in the United States (*World of Work Report*, March 1977, p. 25).

Scanlon plans vary in practice, but there are three defining characteristics. One is a set of committees to communicate problems and develop ideas for improving efficiency. Another is a formula for distributing money to a group of employees in proportion to measured improvements in productivity. The plan is therefore designed to promote productive collaboration in a group of employees, and an equitable distribution of gains from higher productivity. The durability of the Scanlon concept and the number of companies that have adopted some form of it, including some unionized plants, are evidence that the plan has been effective, at least in some organizations.

The third element of the Scanlon plan is the least concrete, but nevertheless essential. In their practical handbook, Moore and Ross call it "the philosophy and practice of cooperation." This includes sharing knowledge and information between employees and management. Ultimately, it may amount to "the merging of personal goals with those of the organization," so that employees "desire to make higher levels of contributions to the attainment of organizational goals" (p. 4). Within the structure provided by the committees and the productivity bonus, the cooperative ethic and spirit reinforce an employee's intrinsic motivation to do good work.

Donnelly Mirrors: A Success Story

One well-publicized story of a successful Scanlon plan is at Donnelly Mirrors, Inc., the major producer of rearview mirrors for automobiles. Donnelly had instituted a Scanlon plan in 1952, but in the late 1960s, like many companies, Donnelly was finding its existing motivational strategy not as effective as management wanted. The Scanlon committees were felt not to be generating enough suggestions. In 1967 a new man, Robert J. Doyle, was hired as director of personnel and organizational development. The company also contracted with the Institute for Social Research at the University of Michigan for a consultant in organizational development, Stephen C. Iman (Rush, 1973, p. 44). These two facilitated and evaluated the reorganization of the Scanlon committees into "semiautonomous" work teams with overlapping membership. Survey results showed production workers felt they had more say or influence over what happened in their departments after these changes (Iman, 1975, p. 226).

Donnelly also changed its pay system in 1970. After separate votes by salaried and hourly employees, the hourly employees were put on salary. Time clocks were abolished. A year later, absenteeism had *dropped* from 5 to 2 percent (Iman, p. 221). Also in 1970, the company and the newly reorganized Scanlon work teams devised workable cost-reduction plans that would save $643,000, then agreed to a constant-percentage increase in base salary—before productivity bonuses—that would amount to $610,000. In 1971, the cost-reduction target to cover increases in base salary was $453,000. Again, actual savings exceeded the target; actual cost reduction was

$511,000 (Iman, pp. 221–222). Apparently the new work teams were succeeding in both suggesting and implementing new efficiency measures, so that higher base salaries did not require lower profits or higher prices for the company's products.

Other apparently hard evidence comes from the productivity index used to compute bonuses under the Scanlon plan. During the 1968–1971 period when Iman and Dyer were working on organizational development, the index of production per unit of direct labor rose at a faster rate than during the preceding four years. The overall index of product quality also improved (Iman, pp. 222–223).

The consensus among managers at Donnelly, according to Iman, was that more effective participation by employees, rather than new equipment, was responsible for most of the gain in productivity. The effects are difficult to separate. When half the gain in productivity was attributed to the organizational development effort, the rate of return on the investment in organizational development was computed to be 220 percent (Iman, p. 224). The investment consisted mainly of the cost of people's time for which the company paid. Donnelly's president concluded:

> *Ours is a less expensive way to manage. We know this because we now have data to back up our impressions. It would be more expensive to operate in an autocratic way because ultimately poor morale, low productivity, a climate of distrust, and worker alienation cost a lot more.* (Quoted in Rush, p. 50)

Limits of the Scanlon Plan

Successful as far as they have gone, motivational programs like those at Donnelly Mirrors still have definite limits. Management, as agent for the company's owners, retains control over essential information and decisions. Even in a company like Donnelly Mirrors, maintaining trust between management and employees requires continual effort and sensitivity. For example, in an article on the merits of the Scanlon plan, Donnelly's Robert Doyle discussed the problem of constructing a formula for the productivity bonus ratio:

> *The skills needed to determine the ratio are honesty, common sense and arithmetic. Honesty is needed to avoid another bad job on the balancing act [between the interests of stockholders, employees, and customers]. If the company needs X percent for dividends and Y percent for growth, do not allow X + 1 percent for dividends and Y + 2 percent for growth, because "what the employees don't know won't hurt them." The average employee on the production line knows that*

he can't understand the company's accounting figures. He further
assumes that accountants deliberately make them complex. He gener-
ally concludes from this that management is hiding something from
him. He does not trust the information he gets from management to
begin with, so if you want him pulling with you instead of against you,
do not give him any more distrust ammunition than he already has.

Evidence that Scanlon plans do not always succeed in establishing trust between employees and management appeared in a 1968 survey of 2,636 employees in 21 plants with Scanlon plans. There were persistent negative feelings that the plan was "a way for management to get more out of the workers" (Goodman, Wakeley, and Ruh, 1972, p. 28). The authors of the survey concluded that these feelings persisted because some organizations were not successful in putting the plan's *philosophy* into practice.

Historically, critics of capitalism have argued that the conflict between a firm's owners and employees is irreconcilable. Carnoy and Shearer (1980), for example, summarize the "radical view" that

. . . worker dissatisfaction emanates from the very maximization of the
return to capital that lies at the basis of capitalist decision making. So
the capitalist definition of "efficiency" includes worker well-being, ful-
ler employment, and higher output only when these are consistent with
increasing returns to capital. In this view, improving the "quality" of
working life without giving workers control of production and invest-
ment decisions might make job conditions better, but it would not
eliminate the process by which managers try to keep wages low relative
to productivity. (p. 130)

Carnoy and Shearer advocate ownership and control of enterprises by the people who work in them, and they provide an informative discussion of means toward this end.

Being one's own boss is part of the traditional American dream, and, in fact, there have been successful examples of employee-owned companies in the United States. (See Zwerdling, 1977; Russell, Hochner, and Perry, 1977; P. Bernstein, 1976.) If there is still a widespread desire among working people to own and control the organizations that employ them, this desire is more likely to be satisfied in an economy with sustained full employment. And the point of this chapter is that sustaining full employment will be more feasible if existing organizations adopt appropriate strategies for managing human resources.

Employee Motivation and National Policy to Increase Productivity

There are many other published examples of employers' efforts to enhance employee motivation by emphasizing the psychological and material rewards of work well done, rather than relying on the threat of termination (O'Toole, 1973; Katzell and Yankelovich, 1975; Glaser, 1976; Davis and Trist, 1974; Davis and Cherns, 1975; Rush, 1971 and 1973; *World of Work Report*). The *Work in America* report to the Secretary of Health, Education and Welfare in 1972 (O'Toole, 1973) asserted that "the redesign of work, accompanied with profit sharing, has a high potential for increasing productivity" (p. 129), and thereby for reducing inflation and unemployment. The "overwhelming majority" of 434 chief executive officers of U.S. corporations surveyed by William Mercer also think that "quality of work life and increased employee satisfaction can help raise the rate of productivity" (*World of Work Report*, February 1981, p. 16).

Economists' Traditional Skepticism of Psychological Influences on Productivity

Economists have traditionally been skeptical that psychological characteristics of jobs affect aggregate productivity, inflation, or employment. Glen Cain, an eminent labor economist, has written:

I confess that I do not understand the analytical distinction between a lack of good jobs and a lack of jobs . . . [Workers of different kinds] are unemployed because the jobs that are known and available to them are not acceptable for a variety of reasons that appear sound to them (and probably would to us, if we knew all the circumstances) . . . [T]he fundamental similarity of the unemployment situation . . . is that the jobs available at the time are not good enough—a rough restatement of the substantive meaning of the census definition of "unemployment"—or, to use an old-fashioned term, "involuntary unemployment." (p. 1238)

Cain recognized that some jobs may have undesirable characteristics, including "employment instability, low pay, poor working conditions, and limited fringe benefits." Similarly, Eli Ginzberg, who predicted that "the availability of good jobs will become a central issue of public policy," nevertheless defined "good" only in terms of "wages, working conditions, fringe benefits, job security, and opportunities for advancement" (Ginzberg, 1977, pp. 48–49). Since wages and other favorable elements tend to go together, Ginzberg resorted to earnings as the most reliable indicator of a good job (Ginzberg, 1979, p. 36).

These statements reveal one of the reasons why economists traditionally have downplayed psychological aspects of jobs. They have not seen the psychological quality of employment in any way *causing* variation in the quantity of employment. They have seen it only as an effect of the quantity of jobs available—and a hard-to-measure effect at that—so they have simply not considered it necessary to include quality of work life as an explanatory variable.

Since quality of employment does not enter into conventional economic theories of productivity or employment, those theories do not treat it as a major policy variable. A 1981 report by economists in the U.S. Congressional Budget Office, for example, described policies by which the federal government might attempt to restore faster growth in productivity. Most of the report dealt with capital accumulation, saving, and physical technology. In one chapter, on policies to improve labor quality, the C.B.O. economists merely noted that "more cooperation between labor and management in matters relating to productivity may offer some promise," and mentioned the Scanlon plan (p. 62).

Economists' Recent Attention to Psychological Factors

Nevertheless, a growing number of contemporary economists have begun to treat employees' effort as a variable in their analysis (for examples, see Hall, Lazear, Okun, D.M. Gordon, Oster, Williamson, Thurow). They have recognized that a rational employer must take account of how the implicit or explicit features of an employment contract are likely to affect a rational employee's level of effort. The analysis in this chapter is a direct extension and elaboration of these ideas.

Conclusion

This chapter makes the case that psychological aspects of work do cause changes in productivity. This is most easily seen in individual organizations, but the behavior of productivity in large sectors of the economy over time is also consistent with this idea. In particular, as we have seen, the job security effect can account for some of the slow-down in productivity growth when a continuing economic expansion makes jobs relatively plentiful. Slower productivity growth pushes up costs and prices, triggering responses by employers and the government which lead to slower expansion and higher unemployment. This has definite implications for economic policy: Sustaining full employment will become easier if growth in productivity can be motivated by the psychological and economic rewards of work well done, so that economic contraction and unemployment are not required to restore rapid growth in productivity. By reducing the necessity of relying on the threat of layoffs to keep productivity growing, improving the psychological quality of employment will help increase the quantity of employment that is possible in the long run.

The next chapter describes some of the practical difficulties in improving the quality of employment. Contrary to Cain's assertion, creating more jobs does *not* automatically create more good jobs. Not all employers respond to labor shortages by letting employees take more responsibility and giving them a "piece of the action." But low unemployment rates or layoff ratios do create a more favorable economic climate for such changes.

Chapter 3

HOW FULL EMPLOYMENT
FAVORS CREATION
OF GOOD JOBS

"Improving the quality of work life is a desirable management goal even if it doesn't increase productivity," according to more than 7 out of 8 managers and union officials surveyed by Katzell and Yankelovich (p. 118). In addition, as explained in the previous chapter, creating more intrinsically motivating work may increase productivity and permit a reduction in the long-run rate of unemployment that can be sustained without accelerating inflation. But redesigning work in actual, ongoing organizations requires a substantial commitment of time and effort. Under what conditions is this commitment likely to occur? Will it increase? Who will decide?

First, some definitions. Any work that is here called intrinsically motivating includes at least some effort made without direct external inducement or threat, material or social, actual or imagined. This effort may express a commitment to personal or professional standards of quality or morality. Richard Walton's "high-commitment work systems" are designed to encourage this kind of effort. Their success depends on commitment, including moral commitment, wherein "people try hard to meet goals" and "don't abuse privileges" (Walton, 1980, p. 212). Intrinsic motivation also may include curiosity, challenge, amusement, or the pleasure of exercising a skill.

This kind of effort does not happen in organizations where employees feel threatened or resentful. It requires a generally high quality of working life—here this phrase means whatever is required in a given organization to allow for intrinsic motivation. If the employees are already on the payroll, their unique characteristics have to be taken into account. That is why improving QWL has to begin with a careful assessment of the opportunities and obstacles specific to the individual organization.

The Costly Process of Job Redesign

The process of creating more intrinsically motivating work is time-consuming, and the outcome is not entirely predictable. One description of the process, by J. Richard Hackman, is contained in a report for the U.S. Department of Labor on "work redesign"— defined as "the alteration of specific jobs (or interdependent systems of jobs) with the intent of increasing both the quality of the work experience of employees and their on-the-job productivity" (Hackman, 1975, p. 4). Hackman warns what can happen when sufficient planning or commitment is lacking.

> *Over the last two years my associates and I have visited numerous organizations where work redesign activities were being planned, implemented, or evaluated. We have talked with large numbers of employees, managers, and internal and external consultants. In several cases, we have made quantitative assessments of the effects of work redesign projects.*
>
> *What we have seen is not encouraging. If our observations are representative, job enrichment projects are failing at least as often as they are succeeding. (Note: In interpreting the observations reported here it is important to understand that we have not researched the "superstar" change projects, such as the Topeka plant of General Foods or the Kalmar plant of Volvo. None of our studies was conducted at a new plant, designed, staffed, and managed in accord with the freshest precepts of behavioral science. Instead, we focused on "regular" organizations, organizations struggling to determine how one can reap the purported benefits of job enrichment.) And the reasons for the failures, in many cases, appear to have more to do with the way planned changes are implemented in organizations than with the intrinsic merit of the changes themselves. Again and again we have observed good ideas about the redesign of work die because the advocates of change were unable to gain acceptance of their ideas, or because unexpected roadblocks led to early termination of the change project. (pp. 75–76)*

To increase the chances for success, Hackman offers six guidelines for implementing changes in jobs: (1) carefully diagnose prior to any redesign whether change is in fact feasible, including whether employees and managers are ready; (2) make sure that jobs really change, which includes dealing with the bureaucratic "personnel-and-job-description apparatus"; (3) prepare contingency plans ahead of time in case things go wrong; (4) continuously evaluate the effects of change; (5) make sure at the outset that managers and union leaders (if any) understand the project and have a commitment to it; and (6) involve employees in the process of change (pp. 76–93). The message is clear: In order for work redesign to succeed, a lot of people have to give it substantial time and attention.

The cost of creating more intrinsically motivating work may also include the time and effort required to make other changes that support the redesign of jobs. Generally, job redesign will improve motivation and productivity only if employees are not already dissatisfied with basic pay, job security, fringe benefits, working conditions, social relations, and other so-called "hygiene" factors (Herzberg, Mausner, and Snyderman, 1959). If employees feel they are being maltreated by the organization, they will not respond positively to more challenge, variety, autonomy, and responsibility in their work. But the cost of eliminating such prior problems could be seen as prohibitive in some organizations.

Importance of Sharing Productivity Gains

In order for job redesign to succeed, there must also be a mechanism enabling employees to share in any productivity gains. According to a 1972 Harris poll, 67 percent of the public agreed that "Companies benefit from increased productivity at the expense of workers," and only 23 percent disagreed. Among hourly wage workers, 80 percent agreed and 14 percent disagreed. The same poll found 70 percent of the public believed stockholders benefit "a lot" from increased productivity, and 68 percent thought management does. But only 20 percent believed employees benefit significantly from increased productivity (National Commission on Productivity, 1973, pp. 87–88). These attitudes may make employees unwilling to participate in job redesign without explicit sharing of the economic gains, even if they agree with the changes.

This kind of resistance was evident in a survey of big-city municipal workers who were asked how much they would like various hypothetical changes, including both personal benefits, such as more time off, and changes in the job that would allow more involvement and participation. Many said they would approve of changes in the job itself as much as changes in personal benefits, but they were more willing to trade a bigger increase in pay for the personal benefits than for changes in the job. The explanation given by some respondents was that the proposed changes in the job would probably increase their productivity, and they did not think they should have to pay for this even though it was something they would like (Stern, 1978).

A similar result was obtained by the 1977 Quality of Employment Survey from a national sample of employed adults. Only 25 percent said they would rather have "more interesting work" than a 10 percent pay raise, even though previous surveys found interesting work was "very important" to the large majority of workers (Quinn and Shepard, p. 66). Only 17 percent said they would give up a 10 percent pay raise to obtain more freedom to decide how to do their work. In contrast, 54 percent said they would give up the 10 percent raise for better retirement benefits, and 48 percent would do it for more paid vacation days (Quinn and Staines, p. 57). Though these comparisons are hypothetical and somewhat imprecise, the responses clearly indicate that employees are reluctant to give up pay in order to have their jobs redesigned. To the contrary, if job redesign is supposed to increase productivity, employees expect to be paid *more*. As Katzell and Yankelovich put it, "Job redesign is likely to work best when everyone involved stands to share equitably in resulting financial benefits" (p. 30).

Katzell and Yankelovich considered the gain-sharing principle so important that they placed it at the top of their summary list of six "critical ingredients" for improving QWL and productivity:

a. *Financial compensation of workers must be linked to their performance and to productivity gains.*
b. *Workers and work must be matched so as to create a work situation which workers will see as capable of meeting their needs and expectations, and where they will have the capabilities and resources to be successful.*
c. *For workers who desire it, their work should provide opportunity for full use of their abilities, making a meaningful contribution, having challenging and diversified duties, and being responsible for others.*

    d. Workers at all levels must have inputs to plans and decisions affecting their jobs and working lives.

    e. Appropriate resources, including work methods and equipment, must be provided to facilitate workers' performance and minimize obstacles to carrying out their jobs.

    f. Adequate "hygiene" conditions must exist, including competent and considerate supervision, fair pay and fringe benefits, job security, good working conditions, and sound employee relations. (pp. 38–39)

Much of this list, which the authors point out is not necessarily complete, overlaps a set of eight criteria proposed by Richard Walton (1973) for defining QWL. Walton's list also includes elements such as protection for employees' rights (including privacy, free speech, and due process) and a balance between work demands and personal responsibilities, especially family. Walton also asserted the value of employees' perceiving the work organization as "socially responsible."

Estimating Actual Costs of Job Redesign

These lists have been proposed as long-term agendas for organizational change. The cost of instituting such extensive changes has not been estimated, but some data have been reported on the cost of more limited job redesign programs. One study of 58 business organizations that initiated formal job enrichment programs found that the average outlay to design and implement the program was $1,075 for each employee whose job was being altered. In addition, each employee received training that required an average of 12.5 days and a direct cost (for instructors, etc.) of $283 per employee. In some organizations, levels of compensation were also increased as employees took on new responsibilities. Finally, temporary declines in output occurred in about a third of the cases while changes were being implemented. Where this "Valley of Despair" was encountered, the average deterioration in productivity was 14 percent over a period of 2.5 months (Alber, 1978). These figures imply that the average employer can expect the initiation of a job enrichment program to cost approximately $2,000 per employee involved.

The Possible Payoffs to Employers

Improving QWL could conceivably yield the following kinds of economic benefits to employers:

- Lower wage scales;
- Reduction in direct cost of training due to reduction in turnover;
- Increase in output per employee-hour, at a given standard of quality;
- Increase in quality of output.

The possibility of a lower wage scale as a result of improving QWL is suggested by the following report:

> *When Arthur King III was laid off two years ago from his production job at a textile factory in Kingston, N.C., he found another job at an Eaton Corp. plant in nearby Greenville. His new job paid nearly $100 a week less than the $300 he had been making. Yet when he was recalled to the textile plant a month later, he decided to stay at Eaton. The reason: The 26-year-old King, a high school graduate, found the Eaton plant to be "a whole lot less regimented" than the factory where he had worked before. . . . "In the other factory, I felt like someone was standing over me all the time, making me nervous," King says. "Here I can concentrate and get more done." (Business Week, May, 23, 1977, p. 80)*

The immediate payoff to Eaton Corporation in this case is a saving in wages. Evidently this employee is willing to work for substantially less because the QWL is better—a decision entirely consistent with the classical theory of wages propounded by Adam Smith and his intellectual heirs. Smith saw five main reasons why earnings varied among occupations. The first was "the agreeableness or disagreeableness of the employments themselves." In an economy where individuals can freely choose among occupations, more agreeable jobs should tend to pay less, and disagreeable jobs should pay more (other things being equal). For example, according to Smith, "the trade of a butcher is a brutal and odious business; but it is in most places more profitable than the greater part of the common trades" (p. 100).

Although the anecdote from Eaton Corporation suggests that Smith's theory has some practical relevance, contemporary economists have *not* found consistent evidence that wage differences compensate for variations in the "agreeableness" of different jobs.

Risk of death is an exception: Several studies have found that jobs where there is greater risk of death do tend to pay more, other things being equal. But even here the estimates vary widely. In different samples, the estimates of extra wages that employers pay to compensate a thousand workers for the possibility of one additional death among them range from 0.2 to 3.5 million dollars. In other words, estimates of possible wage savings from reducing the risk of death by one in a thousand vary widely (R. Smith, 1979). Attempts to estimate how much money employers can save by making work less physically taxing or more psychologically rewarding have been even less enlightening. Several studies have come out with "wrong" signs, implying that employees would actually have to be paid *more* to accept better QWL (R. Smith, 1979; R.E.B. Lucas, 1977). In fact, as the Alber study found, some job enrichment programs may entail higher compensation costs as jobs are upgraded. The Eaton Corporation may have reduced compensation costs through improved QWL, but generally employers cannot count on this immediate payoff.

If organizations were fully efficient, actual wage patterns would correspond more closely to Adam Smith's theory. Full efficiency means that an organization has already done everything possible to improve QWL without hurting productivity, and to increase productivity without sacrificing QWL. Any changes in the organization at this point would have to advance one objective at the expense of the other. Efficient organizations competing for employees would create some range of choice, with some organizations offering relatively high pay and low QWL, and other organizations offering better QWL but lower pay. If an organization offered more of both, it would attract employees from other companies, which would then have to increase their own offers of pay or QWL. Classical economic theory presupposes a long-run tendency toward efficiency, because inefficient companies should be driven out of business. In the long run, if two employers are competing for the same employees and one offers better QWL, the other must offer higher pay.

But those who advocate efforts to improve QWL assume that many organizations are *not* fully efficient in actuality. And in fact opportunities *do* exist in many organizations for increasing both QWL and productivity—and for increasing pay along with productivity. Case study after case study has documented this possibility. Many companies simply have not reached the point where it is necessary to sacrifice QWL for long-run productivity or vice versa. Such employers can improve their ability to recruit and retain employees by offering higher pay along *with* better QWL. As already noted, this also makes it easier to get employees involved in improving QWL. Therefore, companies generally do not count on lower wage scales to offset the cost of improving QWL.

Evidence of Benefits to Employers

Instead, employers look for payoffs in the form of lower training costs resulting from lower turnover, gains in average quantity of output per employee or per hour, and possibly improvements in output quality as well. Such payoffs often do occur. For example, in Alber's sample of 58 companies that undertook job enrichment, 47 reported lower turnover, with an average reduction of 18 percent. Since the average cost of replacing an employee who quits was reported to be more than $2,000, the savings to companies are substantial if maintained over time. In addition, 50 of the 58 companies reported increased production, averaging 21 percent, and nearly half of the 58 also reduced the size of their work force. The reductions all occurred through transfer, promotions, or normal attrition; no employees were fired or laid off as a result of the job enrichment program. (The issue of job security in this context is discussed in the next section.) Among the reasons for increased productivity were fewer machine breakdowns and less time lost due to accidents or absenteeism. (Productivity is output per hour paid, not per hour worked.) Changes in employees' attitudes were generally positive, and this probably also played a part in improving productivity.

Risk to Managers

Unfortunately, none of these payoffs is a sure thing. Even the theories of job redesign are far from certain. Some of the best research on job design has been criticized for failing to distinguish clearly between objective characteristics of jobs and the perception of those characteristics by employees (Roberts and Glick). The research literature generally consists of partial results based on a variety of psychological and organizational theories (Parnes, 1978; Williams, 1976).

A manager who takes responsibility for improving QWL is therefore in a risky position. The costs—planning, training, slower production while changes are made—are up front. But the payoff appears only after some time, if at all. Meanwhile, the responsible manager often has to defend the project against others in the organization who may not believe the theory to begin with. "The worst enemy that quality of work life has is the impatience for quick and finite results," according to the director of QWL programs at AT&T (*Business Week*, May 11, 1981, p. 98).

If managers are not in a position to take the necessary risk, advances in QWL will not occur. Katzell and Yankelovich summarized the problem:

> *To advance the dual objective of enhancing quality of working life and economic performance simultaneously, large scale changes have to be introduced into the workplace before results become visible, measurable, and demonstrably worth the effort. Yet, due to a combination of inadequate knowledge, resistance to change, suspicion of motives and weakness of commitment, changes must be introduced slowly and cautiously. But if the changes are too slow and too cautious, there is a real danger that the objective may never be reached.* (p. 41)

How a Slack Economy Inhibits Investment in Job Redesign

The commitment to improving QWL appears to diminish among both employers and employees when unemployment rates are high. For employers, there is simply less need to bother with the complexity and uncertainty of redesigning jobs and organizational structures when there are plenty of qualified people looking for work. Just as wages on average do not increase as rapidly, neither does QWL improve when labor market conditions give employers more bargaining power relative to employees.

For example, in 1973, when the overall unemployment rate was 4.9 percent, General Motors agreed with the UAW to establish a National Committee to Improve the Quality of Worklife "to discuss, develop, and implement programs for improving the quality of working life" (Bluestone, 1977, p. 8). But when unemployment went up to 8.5 percent in 1975—the highest rate since the 1930s—GM's enthusiasm diminished. Reportedly, "the recession set the program back several years" (O'Toole, 1977, p. 100).

Another case is the General Foods pet food plant in Topeka, Kansas. Built in 1971, it has often been cited as a leading American example of how job redesign can contribute to QWL and higher productivity (O'Toole, 1973; Walton, 1980). After the 1974–1975 recession, however, there was reported to be a growing reaction against the ideas embodied in the Topeka plant, on the part of managers elsewhere in the General Foods organization (*Business Week,* March 28, 1977, pp. 78–82). Lyman Ketchum, who oversaw planning of the Topeka plant and who went on to promote these ideas throughout General Foods, later wrote a convincing description of how the risk inherent in such efforts creates stress for managers and inhibits change (Ketchum, 1975).

Deterioration of QWL with Increased Unemployment

More general evidence, reported by employees themselves, suggests how QWL can actually deteriorate when unemployment rises. The evidence comes from three national surveys conducted by the Institute for Social Research at the University of Michigan in 1969, 1973, and 1977. Overall unemployment rates in those three years were 3.5, 4.9, and 7.0, respectively. Accordingly, the surveys found employees reporting they had less choice in the job market in 1973 than in 1969, and still less in 1977 than in 1973. Table 3.1

Table 3.1   Reported Degree of Difficulty Finding a Job Comparable to Present One, 1969, 1973, 1977

About how easy would it be for you to find a job (with another employer*) with approximately the same income (and fringe benefits*) you now have?

	Percentage†		
Ease of Finding a New Job	*1969 (N=1301)*	*1973 (N=2071)*	*1977 (N=2254)*
Very easy	—	27.5%	22.4%
	(40.3%)	(27.0)	(20.1)
Somewhat easy	—	35.6	35.6
	(29.4)	(35.7)	(36.9)
Not easy at all	—	36.9	41.9
	(30.3)	(37.2)	(43.0)

SOURCE: Quinn, Robert P., and Graham L. Staines. *The 1977 Quality of Employment Survey.* Ann Arbor, MI: Institute for Social Research, University of Michigan, 1979, p. 170. Reprinted with permission of the publisher.

* This phrase was omitted for self-employed workers.

† 1969 data were obtained only from wage and salaried workers. Parenthetical entries for all three years are based on subsamples of waged and salaried workers; other 1973 and 1977 entries are based on the full samples.

shows the percentages of employees who said it would be easy or hard to find another job with the same pay and benefits in those years.

The same surveys also included a set of questions about various aspects of respondents' present jobs. For the most part, reported benefits were slightly less available in 1973 than in 1969, and less available in 1977 than in 1973. (Table 3.2 shows the actual percentages.) The main exception to the overall pattern of decline was in relations with coworkers: The 1977 sample reported more opportunities to make friends on the job. Perhaps this represents a tendency for employees to give each other more support to compensate for less supportive supervision, a faster pace of work, and fewer conditions ("challenge" factors) that can enhance intrinsic motivation.

These survey findings are consistent with the view that, when labor market conditions give more bargaining power to employers, they can put more pressure on employees, relying more on the threat of firing and less on sophisticated strategies for eliciting intrinsic motivation. And, in fact, productivity did grow faster in 1977 and 1973 than in 1969 (see Table 2.2). On the other hand, the apparent decline in QWL was accompanied by an increase in reported availability of fringe benefits and a decrease in severity of work-related illnesses and injuries (Quinn and Staines, 1979, pp. 58–59, 123). There was also a reported increase in employees' control over whether they worked overtime (p. 91), but this could simply reflect a reduction in employers' demand for overtime work in a slower economy.

Given that some of the more tangible benefits from work did not appear to decline, it is possible that the reported decline in QWL was a product of rising expectations among employees rather than a sign of any actual deterioration. However, Graham Staines, one of the survey directors in 1977, rejected this explanation after concluding that the available measures of unmet expectations in the surveys did not account for the trend. Staines also determined that the trend was not attributable to changing demographic composition of the work force. Because survey respondents did not report deterioration of some of the more "objective" job characteristics but did report deterioration on more global measures of satisfaction, Staines concluded that the reported decline in more "subjective" aspects of working life may have been due mainly to "a much broader social malaise, a general and growing disaffection with many or even most of this country's major institutions—political, eco-

Table 3.2   Reported Presence of Various Job Characteristics, 1969, 1973, 1977

Through the "card sort" technique the worker was asked to indicate how true each of the following statements was of his or her job.

		Percentage*			
Statement	Base N	Very True	Some- what True	Not too True	Not at All True
Comfort					
I have enough time to get the	1505	45.9	36.5	11.7	5.9
job done.	2063	41.3	40.3	13.7	4.8
	2244	31.2	44.7	16.8	7.2
The hours are good.	1500	56.7	23.9	10.0	9.4
	2046	51.0	27.5	12.2	9.2
	2241	42.8	33.7	13.9	9.5
Travel to and from work is	1497	61.5	20.7	9.4	8.5
convenient.	2038	59.1	23.5	10.5	7.0
	2222	52.1	26.9	12.5	8.5
The physical surroundings are	1505	48.3	28.4	14.7	8.6
pleasant.	2051	41.6	31.9	18.4	8.1
	2240	35.0	36.7	19.4	8.9
I can forget about my personal	1496	38.0	33.0	16.9	12.2
problems.	2006	31.9	36.1	19.6	12.3
	2230	20.6	38.3	24.7	16.4
I am free from the conflicting	1494	35.3	33.7	19.3	11.7
demands that other people make	2026	22.6	34.6	27.3	15.5
of me.	2217	12.9	33.7	31.2	22.2
I am not asked to do excessive	1491	43.1	31.5	14.8	10.5
amounts of work.	2036	34.2	37.0	16.9	11.8
	2219	27.9	38.6	19.2	14.3
Challenge					
The work is interesting.	1510	63.4	22.1	8.9	5.7
	2066	60.9	21.9	11.6	5.6
	2246	52.7	28.3	12.1	6.9
I have an opportunity to de-	1507	45.8	24.1	16.1	14.1
velop my own special abilities.	2057	42.9	26.8	18.9	11.4
	2241	31.8	32.4	21.4	14.4
I can see the results of my work.	1509	65.1	24.4	7.2	3.2
	2065	63.9	24.9	8.4	2.8
	2244	56.5	29.2	11.5	2.8
I am given a chance to do the	1504	45.4	26.5	15.5	12.6
things I do best.	2049	40.9	29.8	16.8	12.5
	2239	30.7	33.4	21.8	14.1

Table 3.2 (continued)

		Percentage*			
Statement	Base N	Very True	Some-what True	Not too True	Not at All True
I am given a lot of freedom to	1512	53.7	25.5	12.7	8.1
decide how I do my own work.	2062	50.0	30.3	12.2	7.5
	2248	40.1	32.7	18.7	8.5
The problems I am expected to	1497	38.5	33.0	17.2	11.2
solve are hard enough.	2045	33.5	34.7	20.2	11.5
	2225	22.4	36.2	26.3	15.1
Financial Rewards					
The pay is good.	1503	40.3	32.7	15.4	11.6
	2061	40.7	34.6	14.7	10.0
	2246	27.2	38.0	20.2	14.6
The job security is good.	1498	54.9	24.6	10.0	10.5
	2056	52.7	26.8	11.9	8.7
	2241	41.6	33.7	15.6	9.1
My fringe benefits are good.	1294†	41.8	25.7	13.3	19.2
	1804†	43.7	25.7	13.5	17.1
	1943†	32.5	32.2	15.0	20.3
Relations with Co-workers					
The people I work with are	2029	61.4	30.7	6.0	1.9
friendly.	2228	57.0	35.1	6.6	1.2
I am given a lot of chances to	1500	56.5	24.3	13.0	6.2
make friends.	2062	51.5	27.4	16.1	5.0
	2236	56.6	28.4	11.5	3.4
The people I work with take a	2032	34.1	38.5	19.2	8.2
personal interest in me.	2227	29.3	40.9	22.0	7.8
Resource Adequacy					
I have enough information to	1507	64.0	28.3	6.1	1.7
get the job done.	2069	62.6	31.2	4.7	1.4
	2236	51.8	39.9	6.4	1.8
I receive enough help and	1505	59.5	27.6	8.8	4.1
equipment to get the job done.	2046	56.6	31.3	8.4	3.8
	2232	44.7	37.0	12.2	6.0
I have enough authority to do	1505	66.7	24.4	6.6	2.3
my job.	2055	64.0	26.3	7.2	2.5
	2238	53.0	36.2	7.7	3.0

Table 3.2   (continued)

Statement	Base N	Percentage* Very True	Some- what True	Not too True	Not at All True
My supervisor is competent in	1287†	60.3	25.6	8.4	5.7
doing his/her job.	1802†	59.2	27.0	9.3	4.5
	1937†	49.6	31.5	12.8	6.1
My responsibilities are	1500	61.7	26.4	8.0	3.9
clearly defined.	2061	59.0	29.5	8.3	3.3
	2241	48.0	37.2	11.1	3.7
The people I work with are	2022	46.2	40.4	9.5	3.9
competent in doing their jobs.	2220	39.2	44.3	13.9	2.6
My supervisor is very con-	1296†	44.8	28.9	15.7	10.6
cerned about the welfare of	1801†	41.1	33.8	17.0	8.1
those under him/her.	1937†	34.1	35.4	19.3	11.3
My supervisor is successful in	1757†	41.5	36.8	15.2	6.4
getting people to work	1930†	31.9	36.6	20.9	10.6
together.					
My supervisor is helpful to me	1808†	51.4	29.1	13.3	6.1
in getting my job done.	1933†	41.6	32.4	18.9	7.0
The people I work with are	2022	45.5	38.8	11.6	4.1
helpful to me in getting my	2222	43.1	38.6	14.3	4.0
job done.					
My supervisor is friendly.	1804†	60.0	27.2	9.3	3.5
	1940†	53.2	30.8	11.4	4.6

Promotions

Statement	Base N	Very True	Some- what True	Not too True	Not at All True
Promotions are handled fairly.	1721†	32.8	30.5	17.1	19.6
	1864†	20.3	30.7	27.3	21.7
The chances for promotion are	1296†	24.3	24.0	21.7	30.0
good.	1781†	20.3	28.4	22.9	28.4
	1909†	15.8	26.2	28.2	29.8
My employer is concerned about	1769†	30.2	29.6	23.3	16.9
giving everyone a chance to	1907†	23.6	31.5	26.4	18.5
get ahead.					

SOURCE: Quinn, Robert P., and Graham L. Staines. *The 1977 Quality of Employment Survey.* Ann Arbor, MI: Institute for Social Research, University of Michigan, 1979, pp. 216–219. Reprinted with permission of the publisher.

* Where there are entries in three rows, they refer respectively to 1969, 1973, and 1977 data; where there are entries in only two rows, they refer respectively to 1973 and 1977 data.
† Includes only wage and salaried workers.

nomic, cultural, educational, and familial" (Staines, p. 44). While this interpretation may be supported by new data, the existing data are equally consistent with the view that, when unemployment rises, employers revert to what Vroom and Deci called a "paternalistic" management style: They make benefits contingent on membership in the organization and rely on gratitude or the threat of firing, rather than the quality of the job experience, to motivate employees.

Employees Resist Productivity Programs When Threatened by Unemployment

High rates of unemployment may also reduce the commitment of employees and unions to QWL improvement programs if these programs are expected to increase productivity, as they usually are. In the Katzell-Yankelovich survey, 78 percent of the union officials agreed that "Job enrichment is a promising strategy for improving productivity" (p. 115). Of the managers, 75 percent concurred. Seventy-four percent of the union leaders (and 72 percent of the managers) also agreed that "Unions are suspicious of job enrichment, but they will support it once they are confident it isn't a productivity gimmick" (p. 122). One reason the union officials hesitate to support job redesign for productivity is the suspicion that employees will not get a fair share of the productivity gains, a problem we have already discussed; job redesign should be accompanied by some mechanism for gain-sharing.

But even with gain-sharing, employees' and unions' resistance to any productivity-improvement program tends to increase when the unemployment rate is high, because job security becomes a more salient issue. The 1972 Harris poll found a majority of hourly wage workers agreed that "Increased productivity means higher unemployment" (National Commission on Productivity 1973, p. 88). Among the public as a whole, 43 percent agreed and 38 percent disagreed, with 19 percent not sure. This belief appears connected to the perception that "For productivity to increase, machines replace workers and a lot of people lose their jobs," a statement with which 69 percent of hourly wage workers, and 59 percent of the general public, agreed.

Increased Productivity Does Not Mean Higher Unemployment

However, the widespread belief that increased productivity necessarily means higher unemployment is not true for the economy as a
whole. It is true that in any one office, shop, or factory, the introduction of labor-saving technology—whether machines or just better
organization—means fewer jobs *if total output stays the same*. And if
jobs are in fact eliminated, there can be obvious hardship for the
people involved unless they have adequate unemployment insurance, access to information about other available jobs, and the opportunity for retraining or relocation assistance. Some employees
already have these safeguards, but some do not. (See National
Center for Productivity and Quality of Working Life, Winter 1977.)

The point is that people are displaced only if total output does not
increase as fast as output per person. The demand for the products of
any one organization or part of an organization may or may not
increase as fast as output per person. This depends in part on the
organization's policy for pricing its products. If demand does grow
fast enough, total employment grows even while productivity increases. For the economy as a whole, keeping total demand growing
fast enough to achieve growth in employment along with growth in
productivity is the task of fiscal and monetary policy. It is not difficult
to accomplish unless fighting inflation becomes more urgent than
providing full employment. And this brings us back to the point
made in Chapter 2: that a higher rate of productivity growth permits
economic policy to bring about *lower* rates of unemployment without aggravating inflation.

Guaranteeing That No Layoffs or Demotions Will Result from QWL Programs

It is easier for employees and unions to take this broader view when
the actual unemployment rate is low enough that protecting jobs is
not a pressing concern. Anxiety about job security tends to under-
mine the trust that is essential to improving QWL along with productivity. Even at the exemplary General Foods plant in Topeka,
persistent concern over job security inhibited some employees from
speaking frankly about each others' performance in work teams. This
hampered the teams' effectiveness (Walton, 1980, p. 227). Generally, when job security is tenuous, a union or a group of employees

faced with a proposed new program to improve productivity and QWL may see this as a no-win proposition. If the new program does not work, management might conclude that the situation is past redemption and eliminate jobs by closing down the operation. If the program does succeed and productivity improves, the result could again be elimination of some jobs, unless demand is growing fast enough. To avoid putting employees in this double-bind, management can provide an explicit guarantee that no one will be laid off or terminated as a result of the program. For example, Donnelly Mirrors has extended such a guarantee to its employees (Iman, p. 222). Similarly, the agreement between AT&T and the Communication Workers for promoting QWL stipulates:

> *Innovations which result from the QWL process will not result in the layoff of any regular employee or negatively affect the pay or seniority status of a union-eligible employee, whether he or she is a participant in the process or not. (World of Work Report,* August 1981, p. 64)

More companies are in a position to extend this kind of guarantee when overall economic activity is expanding. A growing economy also tends to bring lower unemployment rates, so even if employees have no explicit guarantee from their own employer, they would have a better chance of finding jobs elsewhere if they did get displaced as a result of reorganization to improve productivity in their present place of work.

Although conditions of low unemployment are usually more favorable to adoption of programs to improve productivity and QWL, there have been instances where such programs have been adopted to keep a plant from closing or a business from going bankrupt. The original Scanlon plan was created in such a situation. But it does not follow that the way to promote participative strategies is to create economic emergencies. These changes are more likely to succeed if they are carefully planned and calmly implemented.

Since employers and employees can both make a stronger commitment to improving QWL along with productivity when the economy is expanding and the unemployment rate is low, creating this kind of economic climate is a means of improving QWL. Katzell and Yankelovich called this "the most important of all possible legislative targets" for those hoping to advance QWL (p. 50). Since improving QWL and productivity is also a way to sustain economic expansion and low unemployment, there is a definite affinity of interests between those who want better QWL and those who want economic growth and full employment.

The Emerging Coalition for Lower Unemployment, Higher Productivity, and Better Quality of Working Life

When there is less unemployment, pressure for higher wages and other compensation tends to increase. This occurs because employers find it more difficult to recruit and retain qualified workers at existing levels of compensation. When employees are represented by unions and there is less danger of members being laid off, demands for wages and other benefits will tend to be bigger.

Periods of low unemployment also favor creation of more intrinsically motivating work and better QWL. But for an employer who is seeking to fill job vacancies quickly, raising the pay scale is more likely to attract qualified applicants than launching a job-redesign effort. For example, a help-wanted advertisement can more easily describe an attractive salary than an interesting job. Likewise, a union trying to hammer out a collective bargaining agreement that will have the most appeal to members will stick to common-denominator issues like pay, benefits, job security, and physical working conditions. Even though the Quality of Employment survey in 1973 and 1977 found that a majority of union members, both blue- and white-collar, think their unions should put effort into "helping to make jobs more interesting" (Quinn and Staines, 1979, pp. 186–187), a union bargaining team would have great difficulty translating this into contract language in a way that would represent members' different understandings of what is "interesting." As a result, a 1971 survey of collective bargaining contracts found that "formal acceptance of motivational concepts or programs in collective bargaining has been almost nonexistent" (Blum, Moore, and Fairey, 1973, p. 638).

Limitations of ordinary transactional mechanisms—collective bargaining contracts and employers' usual procedures for recruiting—therefore make it more difficult for employees and unions to obtain improvements in QWL than to gain more pay and fringe benefits. When low unemployment tips the balance of bargaining power in their favor, employees and unions generally do not obtain sufficient improvement in QWL to offset the "job security effect" (see Chapter 2). So productivity grows more slowly, or even declines. Slower growth in productivity by itself tends to raise unit labor cost. The more rapid gains in compensation that occur when unemployment rates are low also push up unit labor cost. Rising unit labor cost means less profit per unit of output. Reduced profit margins make firms cut both production and employment, or raise prices. The government then has to fight inflation. Anti-inflation policies tend to cause higher unemployment, and thus tip the balance of bargaining power back in favor of employers. Low unemployment cannot be sustained unless employees and unions can use the opportunity to press for benefits that also promote productivity growth—in particular, more intrinsically motivating work. Since the usual mechanisms by which employers transact business with employees and unions are ill-suited for this purpose, some deliberate, concerted action is necessary.

Role of Labor Organizations in Improving QWL

Concerted action requires organization. Since the mid-1970s various organizations in the United States have been pressing for improved QWL, some of them created expressly for that purpose. Others are well-established organizations that have found it consistent with their existing agenda. Especially prominent among the established organizations are labor unions such as the United Auto Workers. It is worth quoting at some length from an article by UAW vice president Irving Bluestone in the quarterly publication of the AFL-CIO Industrial Union Department:

> *The thrust of a true quality-of-worklife program includes a process in which workers, armed with ample information, exercise the democratic right to participate in making workplace decisions including job structure and design, job layout, material flow, tools to be used, methods and processes of production, plant layout, work environment, etc. In its broadest sense it means decision-making as to how the workplace will be managed and how the worker will effectively have a voice in being master of the job rather than being subservient to it.*
>
> *In labor and management circles alike, a debate is underway revolving around this concept of improving the quality of worklife. As an elected union official, I am a strong advocate of the introduction of quality-of-worklife programs, but the union must be co-equal with management in developing and implementing them. Over time, the structure of work organization will depart from the time-worn ideas of "scientific management" and move inevitably to a recognition that work should be designed to achieve human fulfillment as well as the production of goods and services; and human fulfillment requires the introduction of democratic values into the workplace through participation by the worker in the decision-making process in managing the job.*

In recent years, an increasing number of employers have recognized the need for developing new ideas in structuring work and in relating to the workers. They have been experimenting with various forms of quality-of-worklife programs. In my view, it is vitally important that the union not stand aloof from these developments, but rather assert leadership as co-equals with management in developing and implementing quality-of-worklife programs. For herein lies a meaningful opportunity to move an additional important step toward democratizing the workplace. It would be a serious blunder if the union movement failed to seize this opportunity. Moreover, improving the quality of worklife in the sense I have described is essentially an extension of the basic goals of unionism: achieving that measure of freedom for workers ordinarily denied them in managing their jobs.

Quality-of-worklife programs which are directed toward the human development of the workers, elevating human dignity, and self-fulfillment require mutual, cooperative effort on the part of management and the union. That is why the first programs should be devoted to creating a solid climate of mutual respect between the parties. It is important to understand that hard-line collective bargaining between the negotiating parties continues even while the quality-of-worklife program is in effect. Experience indicates that normal collective bargaining and the introduction of quality-of-worklife programs can exist and succeed side by side. Certain fundamental conditions, however, should prevail when such programs are introduced.

1. *The program should be voluntary and should be fashioned from the bottom up rather than from the top down. Simply to impose a program upon the union and the workers without mutual, cooperative agreement will doom it to failure.*
2. *In the union-management relationship, the parties should develop a mutual respect for each other in their ongoing relationship as honorable participants in the success of the quality-of-worklife program.*
3. *The emphasis should be not on working harder, but rather on enhancing human development and increasing job satisfaction. Either party should be able to cancel the quality-of-worklife program by appropriate notice to the other party, and thus insure that continuation of the program depends on continuing confidence in the intentions and integrity of each other.*
4. *The workers should be assured that they will not perform at an abnormal workpace.*
5. *The workers should be assured that they will not be displaced by reason of the operation of the program.*
6. *The parties should agree that all the terms of the labor agreement will remain in full effect.*
7. *The workers should enjoy some form of reward as the quality-of-worklife program progresses, to be worked out between the union and management.* (Bluestone, 1978, pp. 22–23)

The UAW has played an initiating or cooperating role in several efforts to improve the quality of working life, which exist side by side with "hard-line collective bargaining." These include programs at General Motors under the Joint Committee to Improve the Quality of Work Life (Bluestone, 1977), the Scanlon-type plans established in several Dana Corporation plants (Loftus and Walfish, 1977), and the exemplary, in-depth "Work Improvement Program" at the Harman International plant in Bolivar, Tennessee (Maccoby, 1975).

The UAW is not the only American labor union seeking ways to improve the quality of working life. Others that have joined in concerted action with employers include the United Mineworkers, Teamsters, United Rubber Workers, United Paperworkers, and the International Association of Machinists and Aerospace Workers (National Center for Productivity and Quality of Working Life, February 1976).

Many unions participate in local or national labor-management committees with particular employers. The existence of such a committee does not in itself represent a concerted effort to redesign jobs. In some instances the formation of joint committees has been stimulated by the Federal Mediation and Conciliation Service as part of its overall program to prevent strikes and promote industrial peace (Douty, 1975). Still, the existence of such a committee helps create a climate in which QWL is more likely to be discussed. Machinists' President William W. Winpisinger, who reports that the IAM has entered into more joint written agreements with employers than any other union except the American Federation of State, County, and Municipal Employees, affirms that "at the heart of these agreements has been a concern for productivity and the quality of working life" (Winpisinger, 1978, p. 4).

However, in the debate about union involvement in programs to improve QWL, IAM President Winpisinger has been highly articulate in stating the dangers, drawbacks, and limitations. In 1973 he quipped that job enrichment was "a stopwatch in sheep's clothing" (Calame, 1973). In 1978 he demanded,

Behind all the sophisticated jargon, behavioral experiments and scientific management theories, isn't the objective really just to reduce costs and maximize profits at the expense of the human factor of production? (p. 7)

Winpisinger blamed academics for ignoring the adverse effects on productivity and QWL caused by occupational safety and health hazards, attempts by management to take away basic contract provisions like sick leave and rest periods, the actual or threatened flight of employers to regions or countries where workers are not unionized, and the attack against unions by employers in workplaces and in legislatures. He suggested that studying "management alienation," the source of this "social hostility" by employers, would "provide full employment for behavioralists for the next 50 years or more."

In the adversarial relationship between representatives of employees and representatives of stockholders, as in any relationship where both conflict and cooperation are possible, some individuals will take a hard line and some will seek common ground. The posture of leaders depends on their personalities and on the situation. In labor-management relations, the redesign of jobs may never be as salient an issue as "bread and butter," and in some industries and locations it may never become an issue at all. There will always be conflict between the interests of employees and the interests of stockholders or whoever owns the workplace. Yet those interests also coincide in some ways. This is why many unions, including the Machinists', have joined with employers in concerted efforts to improve both productivity and the quality of life at work.

Other Organizations That Support Improved Productivity and QWL

Efforts by individual companies and unions are now being facilitated by new organizations formed for the express purpose of promoting productivity and the quality of working life. Prominent among these are the American Center for the Quality of Work Life in Washington, D.C.; the American Productivity Center in Houston, Texas; and the Work in America Institute in Scarsdale, New York. These three nonprofit organizations were started in the mid-1970s with funds from governments, unions, and business. As of 1978, there were also several smaller organizations with similar missions, in addition to more than a dozen institutes and centers based at universities (National Center for Productivity and Quality of Working Life, Fall 1978). These new organizations, along with a number of management consulting firms, are attempting to produce new knowledge, increase public awareness, and support efforts to restructure work in specific locations. By creating new communication links among people in different workplaces, these support centers are increasing the likelihood of effective action in each place. In these ways, the new organizations have begun to weave a coalition for change.

The central aims of this informal coalition have been to develop and share knowledge about how to promote productivity and QWL. The formation of national organizations for this purpose also reflects an awareness that promoting productivity and QWL will help eventually to achieve the national goal of full employment without accelerating inflation. At the same time, more groups in this coalition can be expected to advocate keeping unemployment as low as possible in the short run, as it becomes more evident that lower unemployment increases the perceived payoff to job restructuring. Labor unions, of course, traditionally advocate a low-unemployment policy in any event.

This chapter and the preceding one are intended to clarify the common interests of those advocating QWL and those who continue to call for full employment. The remaining two chapters describe some of what an effective coalition might accomplish in the public and private sectors.

Chapter 4

WHAT GOVERNMENTS CAN DO

The federal government can use its fiscal and monetary powers to keep unemployment as low as possible without accelerating inflation. But what if both the rate of inflation and the rate of unemployment keep rising in spite of federal policies? At some point, popular pressure would probably bring about some form of control on prices, wages, and maybe profits. A political coalition that wants to take a strong position in favor of full employment should urge that controls be imposed if the unemployment rate reaches something like 8 or 9 percent.

Governments at all levels can take at least three other kinds of action. First, they can set examples of effective management by using the best known practices for improving productivity and QWL. There is no compelling reason why management in the public sector has to lag behind the private sector, or why it could not sometimes lead. In fact, some notable successes have been achieved in "making government work better," and public employees' unions have responded to taxpayers' revolt by endorsing these efforts. The first part of this chapter reviews some of what has been learned.

Public employment, at least in civil service, has traditionally provided a level of job security like that which would prevail generally in a fully employed economy. Demonstrating how to apply the best known techniques to improving productivity and QWL in regular public employment will therefore provide some lessons to help private enterprises evolve toward full employment.

This suggests a second way for governments at all levels to promote full employment, productivity, and QWL. In addition to adopting the best known management techniques, governments can

Table 4.1   Selected Statistics on Government Expenditure, Employment, and Salaries, 1950–1979

| Year | Government Purchases of Goods and Services, as Proportion of GNP | | | | (5) Wages and Salaries of All Government Employees, as Proportion of All Government Purchases of Goods and Services | Civilians Employed by Government as Proportion of All Civilian Employment | | Indexes of Government Salaries (1967 = 100) | | |
	(1) Total	(2) Non-Defense Total*	(3) Federal Non-Defense	(4) State and Local		(6) Total	(7) State and Local	(8) Avg. Salary of Federal Domestic Employees on General Schedule	(9) Maximum Salary of Firefighters and Police in Cities of 100,000 or More	(10) Avg. Salary of Public Classroom Teachers in Cities of 100,000 or More
1950	13%	8%	2%	7%	59%	12%†	8%†	44	45	49
1960	20	11	2	9	49	13	10	72	72	77
1970	22	15	2	13	53	17	13	130	128	122
1973	21	15	2	13	55	17	13	156	157	149
1976	21	16	3	14	52	17	14	181	193	184
1979	20	15	2	13	49	16	14	221		

SOURCE: *Handbook of Labor Statistics 1980.* Columns 1–4: Table 187; column 5: Tables 187 and 189; columns 6–7: Tables 1 and 100; columns 8–10: Tables 124–126.

* Total in column 2 may differ slightly from sum of columns 3 and 4, due to rounding.
† Data are for 1952.

sponsor efforts to discover better techniques. Given the traditional job security in regular public employment, government agencies are good places to learn more about how to keep employees motivated and productive when employment relationships are expected to last for decades. Toward this end, the possible use of paid sabbatical leave is discussed as an example.

Finally, a third way for governments to help the economy evolve toward sustained full employment is to assist private enterprises that are adopting the desired strategies. A vast number of specific possibilities would be conceivable here. The last section of this chapter describes the general possibilities and a couple of examples.

"Making Government Work Better": Using Public Employment to Demonstrate QWL and Productivity under Conditions of High Job Security

The proportion of employment and economic activity taking place in the public sector was larger in 1979 than in 1950. This growth was in state and local government. Columns 1–4 of Table 4.1 show what happened from 1950 to 1979 to "government purchases of goods and services." These represent the part of gross national product that is spent by governments each year. About half goes for wages and salaries of government employees, as column 5 shows. The rest goes to private businesses that sell products or services to governments. Transfer payments—for example, social security or unemployment insurance benefits—are not included because these are spent by the private individuals or households that receive them. As a proportion of GNP, government purchases of goods and services rose from 13 to 20 percent between 1950 and 1960. Most of the increase in that decade was for defense. But from 1960 to 1979, non-defense spending by governments grew from 11 to 15 percent of GNP, while total government spending rose to 22 and then returned to 20 percent of GNP. Almost all of the increase in non-defense spending occurred at the state and local levels. Accordingly, as column 7 shows, state and local governments also absorbed a rising share of all civilian employment. Over the period from 1950 to 1979, state and local governments approximately doubled their share of total economic activity—from about 7 to 14 percent—as measured by both spending and employment.

This is a disturbing trend for those who see "big government" as a big problem. So is the relatively rapid rise in salaries of public employees. While average gross earnings of production workers in the private sector grew 330 percent in current dollars from 1950 to 1976, columns 8–10 of Table 4.1 show salaries of federal government employees, municipal police and firefighters, and public school teachers rose 411, 429, and 376 percent respectively.

Taxpayers Revolt

In the 1970s, when many households were feeling "ripped off" by rising prices, the general willingness to pay for expanding government or higher salaries for public employees diminished and in some places disappeared. Even though real, spendable earnings were being eroded much more by the rise in prices of privately produced goods and services than by the direct cost of government, the rhetoric of the taxpayers' revolt directed all the outrage against government. This is understandable, since voters cannot affect pricing decisions by private companies—except by imposing price controls—but they can pass referenda or elect politicians to cut taxes and spending by governments.

In June 1978, voters in California passed the famous Jarvis-Gann initiative, Proposition 13, by a two-to-one margin. This amended the state constitution to keep property tax rates from exceeding 1 percent. A Gallup poll in July 1978 found 81 percent of the public in favor of an amendment to the U.S. Constitution requiring the federal government to balance its budget every year (Pechman, 1979, p. 213). No constitutional limit has yet been placed on the size of the federal budget. But, by 1980, 15 states and hundreds of local jurisdictions had put constitutional or statutory limits on their own taxes or spending (*Business Week*, June 23, 1980).

Response by Public Employees' Unions

The main organized force opposing the taxpayers' revolt has been public employees' unions. Unlike the elected or appointed officials who act as top management in the public sector—and who sometimes found during the 1970s that the best way to advance their personal careers was to align themselves with the taxpayers' revolt—the unions representing public employees consistently oppose reduction or limitation of government payrolls.

Public employees' unions grew rapidly during the 1950s, 1960s, and into the 1970s. From 1956 to 1978, while reported membership in all American labor unions grew only 20 percent, from 18.1 to 21.7 million, membership in the public employees' unions quadrupled, from 0.9 to 3.6 million (*Handbook of Labor Statistics 1980*, Table 162). One of the fastest growing public unions was the American Federation of State, County, and Municipal Employees (AFSCME). In the early 1970s, Jerry Wurf, president of AFSCME, was working with other leaders of public employees' unions to consolidate their gains in membership. Their objective was a national "Wagner Act for public employees, guaranteeing . . . the right to join a union, to bargain for decent wages and proper working conditions" (in Flynn, 1975, p. viii).

However, the political climate for public employees' unions deteriorated rapidly as the taxpayers' rebellion mounted in the late 1970s. As recently as 1975, Jerry Wurf could boast about having beaten back an early tax-limitation measure in 1972.

In California our union and NEA [National Education Association, the largest national organization of public employees] worked together to defeat then-Governor Reagan's proposal to write into the state constitution a limit on taxes and spending. This measure, a last gasp of Reaganism, would have had a devastating impact on schools and other public services. (Flynn, pp. vii–viii)

By 1980 it was obvious that the 1972 measure had not in fact been the "last gasp" of taxpayers' revolt. And Ronald Reagan had advanced from "then-Governor" to President-elect.

Faced with this sudden adverse change in the political climate, public employees' unions have naturally tried to defend their previous gains and to extend them where possible. In addition, they have expressed more willingness to share responsibility for "making government work better," as Wurf expressed it in 1976 (Chickering, 1976, p. 181). For example, when a subcommittee of the U.S. House of Representatives held hearings in 1978 on the taxpayers' revolt and fiscal problems of local government, this theme was emphasized in two statements from large public unions. One was by Donald Wasserman, research director of AFSCME:

For its part AFSCME has repeatedly stated its willingness and desire to assist in making local government more productive. Our International President Jerry Wurf has repeatedly challenged local government to join with AFSCME in raising the performance level of local governments—from the elected officials and department heads through rank and file employees. We have said that we are prepared to bargain, negotiate, discuss or consult with local government management on all aspects of the effective and efficient delivery of services, including the productivity of its employees—our members. Unfortunately, local governments generally respond to this challenge only when battling a severe crisis as in the case of New York City, or when an impending crisis looms as in the case of several other cities. There are instances, however, where we have been able to work out productivity arrangements with a number of local governments. These arrangements are not altruistic.

We too have a substantial stake in the survival and viability of local government. We too have a substantial stake in the public's perception of public employees. And, let's face it—that perception is not always positive. (U.S. House, p. 366)

The other statement was by the AFL-CIO Public Employee Department, which comprises unions representing two million local, state, federal, and postal service employees. The statement asserted:

. . . unions and public managers cooperating closely through the collective bargaining system can devise better ways of performing public functions, with an opportunity for workers to participate in the savings resulting from new methods of doing business. One of the key elements to upgrading the quality of government services is involvement of workers. . . .

The National Center for Productivity and Quality of Working Life reported this spring that 55 labor-management committees are functioning in public service. . . .

One aspect of the Center's mission, which has received scant attention, is the quality of working life. That subject warrants careful scrutiny in government service, because it holds the hope of improving significantly the conditions under which government employees complete their tasks. (U.S. House, pp. 595–596)

"Making government work better" can have two meanings, both of which come through in these statements. One is making government operations more cost-effective. The other is making QWL better for public employees. This two-fold response to the taxpayers' revolt would, therefore, promote the same pair of objectives—productivity and QWL—that companies like AT&T and Donnelly Mirrors have been pursuing for some time. As discussed earlier, employers in the private sector are more likely to invest in QWL when the unemployment rate is low and employees have a relative abundance of job options. At such times productivity growth tends to diminish; this is the "job security effect" described in Chapter 2. In the public sector the job security effect is chronic, and productivity of public employees is continually perceived to be low. "Making government work better" could therefore provide valuable lessons for the private sector in how to maintain productivity growth under conditions of high job security.

Job Security and the Problem of Productivity in Government

Since the enactment of civil service laws preventing the wholesale firing of public employees when a new political party wins control of the executive branch, job security has been one of the main advantages of working for the government. This came through clearly in a survey we* did in 1974 in a major northeastern city. The sample, from a large and heterogeneous public employees' union, consisted of all union members in four narrow occupational groups: social service supervisors, nurse's aides, accountants, and college office assistants (secretaries in a public university system). The survey was carried out,† after a year of discussion and pre-testing, from May through July of 1974. At that time, employees in this sample were not yet threatened by fiscal crisis and taxpayers' revolt. We asked, "All in all, how satisfied would you say you are with your job?" Then, "How satisfied would you say you are with each of the following aspects of your job?" Possible responses were: very satisfied, somewhat satisfied, not too satisfied, not at all satisfied. Table 4.2 shows the percentage who indicated they were very satisfied with their job as a whole and with specific aspects of it. More of the accountants and college office assistants declared themselves very satisfied with their job security than with any other aspect of their job. Social service supervisors also rated it among the

---

* The first person plural incorporates several individuals whose assistance in planning, executing, and analyzing the survey was indispensable. They are David Berg, Nancy G. Galuszka, Franklin Lewis, Leslie Petrovics, Ellice Peyton, Charles Whitmore, and Mark Willis.
† The large majority of these four groups were union members. Questionnaires were sent by mail to all accountants, college office assistants (B), and social service supervisors (1) on the union mailing list. The overall response rate from this mailing was 22 percent. To check for non-response bias, we visited several work sites and obtained questionnaires from individuals who had not returned them by mail. Comparison of these "call-back" questionnaires with the "mail-back" sample indicates that the mail-back group over-represented young, white males among the social service supervisors; but there were no consistent differences for accountants or college office assistants. For nurse's aides, we administered the questionnaires through personal interviews rather than by mail.

Table 4.2 Percentage* of Each Occupational Group Responding "Very Satisfied" with Job As a Whole and with Specific Aspects

Aspect of Job	Accountants (N=164)	College Office Assistants (N=214)	Nurses' Aides (N=90)	Social Service Supervisors (N=427)
Job as a whole	8	32	48	11
Pay	4	13	6	6
Fringe benefits	41	54	22	35
Time off	42	46	37	33
Job security	52	69	33	30
Opportunity to get the facts and information necessary to do the job well	8	18	38	3
Opportunity for promotion	2	6	24	1
Opportunity to learn new skills and abilities	1	9	34	3
Opportunity to make friends on the job	15	29	60	19
Opportunity to decide how you do your work	11	32	50	13
Opportunity to use the skills and abilities you have	6	27	44	9
Opportunity to do a variety of things	7	31	34	12
Opportunity to get recognition for your work	3	14	33	5
Opportunity to have an impact on the way things are done	1	15	22	5
Opportunity to get competent supervision	8	19	50	5
Opportunity to use your time as you see fit	11	20	35	10

* Percentage of number responding to each question. N = total number in sample.

most positive aspects of their job. Nurse's aides did not, and for a good reason: they were not covered by civil service rules protecting job tenure.

We also asked, "Compared to jobs held by other people of your age, sex, and educational background, how would you rate your job in terms of . . ." (the items listed in Table 4.2). Again the responses showed that public employees, especially those protected by civil service, do see their jobs as highly secure relative to other jobs for which they might compete.

At the same time, the popular perception of public employees is that they are relatively unproductive. In a 1972 Harris poll, 39 percent of the public said government workers were less productive than average, and only 11 percent said government workers had higher than average productivity. Of 11 groups of workers whose productivity respondents were asked to rate, government workers were rated lowest. The next lowest were repairmen, whose productivity was said to be below average by 24 percent of the people polled, and higher than average by 17 percent. At the high end of perceived productivity were doctors and nurses: their productivity was rated higher than average by 42 percent of the public, and below average by only 9 percent (National Commission on Productivity, 1973, p. 89). These perceptions may or may not be accurate, but they are nevertheless shared by respondents who are in different occupational groups themselves, from professional to unskilled and including union members. This "image problem" of government workers is nothing new. But the growing strength of taxpayers' resistance in recent years is requiring public employees' unions to direct more immediate attention to the problem and to the real, underlying issue of efficiency in government.

Efforts to Improve Productivity in Public Employment

The 1970s produced an abundance of reports describing successful efforts to improve the productivity or efficiency of various groups of public employees. Some of the most informative studies came out of the National Center for Productivity and Quality of Working Life. Legislation creating the Center was enacted in 1975 but unfortunately was allowed to expire in 1978. Before its untimely demise, the Center published a volume of exemplary case studies, demonstrating how six local governments and one state agency had applied conventional management techniques to the problems of measuring outputs, clocking the amounts of time required in various operations, identifying bottlenecks, and generally establishing a clearer connection between objectives and resources (National Center for Productivity and Quality of Working Life, Spring 1977). These case studies tend to confirm reports from other sources (Greiner, 1977; Committee for Economic Development, 1976; Newland, 1972; International City Management Association, 1979; Balk, 1974a) that techniques do exist for improving the efficiency of government agencies, and that they can work if there is a will to use them.

Importance of Commitment by Public Employees, Unions, and Managers

Application of techniques to improve productivity in the public sector, as in the private sector, is most likely to succeed if the commitment to improving productivity is shared by managers and employees. Where a union exists, it must also share this commitment, since otherwise it can hamper attempts to install new procedures, alter job descriptions, and reassign workers. The commitment of employees and unions is especially important in the public sector because managers in the public sector "have neither the control nor the authority of most of their counterparts in business" (Balk, 1974b, p. 320). A group of business leaders studying productivity in government attributed this in part to preoccupation with politics rather than performance.

> *Elected officials generally have little understanding of administration and in any case tend to be more preoccupied with resolving political conflict and building support for the future. This lack of interest in administration among elected officials in turn affects the first ranks of professional managers, who tend to be cautious about attempted improvements that may have political repercussions for their elected superiors and hence for themselves. Thus, it is not surprising that motivation is also weak among managers at lower levels.* (Committee for Economic Development, 1976, p. 41)

In addition, even when public managers have a clear political mandate to improve productivity, they are limited in what they can do, because many public employees are engaged in face-to-face services where they have to make decisions that are both quick and non-routine. To quote the business group again,

*No policy directives or management controls can incorporate the sub-
tlety and detail needed to guide a policeman in dealing with ambiguous or delicate situations or a teacher trying to respond to differing
student needs and problems.* (p. 52)

Evidence of Commitment

Do public employees in fact have any commitment to "making government work better," or are the recent statements by union leaders
only so much public relations? Do union members themselves care
at all about productivity, or are they mainly enjoying their civil
service tenure while waiting to retire on large pensions? It is not
possible to answer these questions for all union members or public
employees. But our survey of public employee union members in a
big city did elicit widespread expressions of interest in redesigning
jobs for better productivity and QWL. We developed a list of job-
redesign proposals by talking with small groups in each of the four
selected occupations. We then presented the list to the entire sample with the question, "How much would you personally like or
dislike each of the following specific proposals for changing your
job?" We tried to ensure that the proposals would be taken seriously
by conducting the survey with the cooperation of the union itself.
The union leadership cooperated actively by providing membership
lists, helping us to arrange interviews, reviewing drafts of our questionnaires, and writing cover letters on union stationery. Though the
union was by no means committed to using the survey results, the
fact that the leaders actively cooperated meant that respondents
could see some possibility that the survey would influence union
policy and therefore their own jobs.

Tables 4.3–4.6 show the responses to the proposed changes. In
each table the first five columns display the percentage distribution
of responses to all the proposed changes for one occupational group.
The next three columns in each table give the percentage distribution of respondents who indicated they would like a proposed
change more than, the same as, or less than they would like having
their working hours reduced by two hours a week. This comparison,
in other words, uses the stated desire for having the two-hour reduction in workweek as a baseline for assessing the stated desires for all
the other proposed changes. Since some of the proposals represented options that some of the respondents already had, the per-

Table 4.3 Accountants' Desire for Changes in Their Job

Proposed Change	Would Like Very Much	Would Like	Would Not Like	Would Dislike Very Much	N.A. or Already Have It	Compared to a 2-Hour Reduction in Work Week, This Proposed Change Would Be:		
						More Desirable	Same	Less Desirable
1. Being on a committee with other accountants, program directors at your location, and other administrators which would meet 2 hours every week during work time to decide how to improve work procedures and conditions where you work.	47%	40%	11%	2%	1%	27%	42%	31%
2. Being allowed to spend up to 2 hours every week during work time acquiring new skills, information, and expertise to help you in your work. You could spend this time reading, gathering information on your own, enrolling in courses, getting together with other accountants to organize training workshops for yourselves, or in any other way that would be useful to you—provided that you keep your supervisor informed of how you are spending this time.	51	38	7	2	1	26	51	23
3. Being allowed to arrive at work any time between 8 and 11 a.m., and to leave at any time between 4 and 7 p.m.—provided you work the same total number of hours *each day* as you do now.	50	25	18	8	0	19	53	28
4. Reimbursement of up to $700 a year for the cost of education or counseling services, whether related to the job or not.	59	29	9	3	0	31	46	23

Table 4.3 (continued)

Proposed Change	Would Like Very Much	Would Like	Would Not Like	Would Dislike Very Much	N.A. or Already Have It	Compared to a 2-Hour Reduction in Work Week, This Proposed Change Would Be:		
						More Desirable	Same	Less Desirable
5. Having the opportunity to submit written proposals for demonstrations of new or improved ways to perform accounting functions. A committee of accountants and administrators would make resources available from a discretionary fund to support the best proposed demonstrations. If you win, you would be in charge of carrying out your own proposal.	35	47	11	2	4	21	45	34
6. Having your working hours reduced by 2 hours a week.	54	31	12	3	1	0	100	0
7. Being allowed to come and go from work at any time you choose—provided you work the same total number of hours *each week* as you do now.	42	18	26	14	1	10	53	37
8. Being part of a team with your supervisor and coworkers which would have the authority to decide as a group how the work is done—provided the total output of work is the same as it is now.	43	38	8	2	9	18	55	27
9. Being allowed to take a whole year off with half pay after every 10 years—with no effect on sick leave, annual leave, or terminal leave.	60	18	11	9	2	23	59	18

Table 4.4 College Office Assistants' Desire for Changes in Their Job

Proposed Change	Would Like Very Much	Would Like	Would Not Like	Would Dislike Very Much	N.A. or Already Have It	Compared to a 2-Hour Reduction in Work Week, This Proposed Change Would Be: More Desirable	Same	Less Desirable
1. Being on a committee with other college office assistants, faculty, administrators, and students which would meet for 2 hours every week during work time to decide how to improve procedures and conditions where you work.	43%	33%	20%	1%	3%	12%	43%	45%
2. Being allowed to spend up to 2 hours every week during work time acquiring new skills, information, and expertise to help you in your work. You could spend this time reading, gathering information on your own, enrolling in courses, getting together with other college office assistants to organize training workshops for yourselves, or in any other way that would be useful to you—provided that you keep your supervisor informed of how you are spending this time.	56	29	11	3	2	13	55	32
3. Being allowed to arrive at work any time between 8 and 11 a.m., and to leave at any time between 4 and 7 p.m.—provided you work the same total number of hours *each day* as you do now. There would be a procedure for coordinating individual schedules.	45	24	17	12	2	9	44	47
4. Reimbursement of up to $500 a year for the cost of education or counseling services, whether related to the job or not.	47	31	13	2	7	7	58	35

Table 4.4 (continued)

Proposed Change	Would Like Very Much	Would Like	Would Not Like	Would Dislike Very Much	N.A. or Already Have It	Compared to a 2-Hour Reduction in Work Week, This Proposed Change Would Be:		
						More Desirable	Same	Less Desirable
5. Having the opportunity to submit written proposals for demonstrations of new or improved ways to perform office functions. A committee of college office assistants and administrators would make resources available from a discretionary fund to support the best proposed demonstrations. If you win, you would be in charge of carrying out your own proposal.	36	40	17	3	5	11	39	50
6. Having your working hours reduced by 2 hours a week.	72	22	2	2	1	0	100	0
7. Having 5 days every year for thorough orientation and training sessions, which would be planned by a committee of college office assistants, administrators, and training consultants.	58	28	9	3	2	15	54	31
8. Being allowed to come and go from work at any time you choose—provided you work the same total number of hours each week as you do now. There would be a procedure for coordinating individual schedules.	40	20	20	10	11	5	52	43
9. Being part of a team with your supervisor and coworkers, which would have the authority to decide as a group how the work is done—provided the total output of work is the same as it is now.	41	29	8	4	18	12	52	36
10. Being allowed to take a whole year off with half pay after every 10 years—with no effect on sick leave, annual leave, or terminal leave.	75	11	3	2	9	16	75	9

Table 4.5 Nurse's Aides' Desire for Changes in Their Job

Proposed Change	Would Like Very Much	Would Like	Would Not Like	Would Dislike Very Much	N.A. or Already Have It	Compared to a 2-Hour Reduction in Work Week, This Proposed Change Would Be:		
						More Desir-able	Same	Less Desir-able
1. Having 10 or 15 minutes at the beginning of your shift, and another 10 or 15 minutes at the end of your shift, for the nurses and aides who are going off duty to tell the nurses and aides who are coming on duty about what is happening with the patients on the ward.	42%	14%	1%	1%	42%	28%	59%	13%
2. Being on a committee with other nurse's aides, doctors, nurses, technicians, and administrators which would meet for 2 hours every week during work time to decide how to improve procedures and conditions in this hospital.	47	40	2	1	10	21	52	27
3. Having the option of working two 4-hour shifts each day, with time off in between to do other things—instead of one continuous 8-hour shift.	3	11	43	40	2	0	17	83
4. Having 5 days with pay every year for thorough orientation and training sessions, which would include topics like emergency procedures, taking vital signs, and communication with patients.	61	31	2	1	4	23	62	15
5. Having work time reduced by 2 hours a week with no cut in pay.	56	37	4	3	0	0	100	0
6. Payment of up to $400 a year for the cost of any education, training, or counseling services, whether related to job or not.	53	38	4	2	2	18	66	16

Table 4.5 (continued)

Proposed Change	Would Like Very Much	Would Like	Would Not Like	Would Dislike Very Much	N.A. or Already Have It	Compared to a 2-Hour Reduction in Work Week, This Proposed Change Would Be:		
						More Desir-able	Same	Less Desir-able
7. Being part of a team with your supervisor and coworkers, which would have the authority to decide as a group how the work is done—provided the total output of work is the same as it is now.	42	31	3	3	20	18	54	28
8. Having a contest every year for nurse's aides in your hospital, where the nurse's aides who write in the best suggestions for improving patient care would win an extra week of paid vacation. The winners would be chosen by a committee of nurses, doctors, and administrators.	50	34	12	3	0	20	47	33
9. Having the option of working different amounts of time on different days—provided you work the same total number of hours *each week* as you do now.	28	33	26	12	1	7	46	47
10. Being allowed to take a whole year off with half pay every 10 years—with no effect on sick leave, annual leave, or terminal leave.	44	30	17	8	1	11	57	32
11. Giving patients a form when they leave the hospital to write down the name of any nurse's aides who have given them extra care. Aides whose names get written down by a lot of patients could get up to 5 extra paid holidays each year. Aides whose names do not get written down by any patients would not get any extra holidays, but no one would lose any time off because of this, and no one's evaluation would be affected.	37	31	18	11	3	15	41	44

Table 4.6   Social Service Supervisors' Desire for Changes in Their Job

Proposed Change	Would Like Very Much	Would Like	Would Not Like	Would Dislike Very Much	N.A. or Already Have It	Compared to a 2-Hour Reduction in Work Week, This Proposed Change Would Be:		
						More Desirable	Same	Less Desirable
1. Being on a committee with other social service supervisors, program directors at your location, and other administrators which would meet for 2 hours every week during work time to decide how to improve procedures and conditions where you work.	46%	35%	11%	3%	5%	29%	41%	30%
2. Being allowed to spend up to 2 hours every week during work time acquiring new skills, information, and expertise to help you in your work. You could spend this time reading, gathering information on your own, enrolling in courses, getting together with other social service supervisors to organize training workshops for yourselves, or in any other way that would be useful to you—provided you keep your supervisor informed of how you are spending this time.	57	29	7	2	5	32	47	21
3. Being allowed to arrive at work any time between 8 and 11 a.m., and to leave at any time between 4 and 7 p.m.—provided you work the same total number of hours each day as you do now. There would be a procedure for coordinating individual schedules.	53	24	14	8	1	27	45	28
4. Reimbursement of up to $700 a year for the cost of education or counseling services, whether related to the job or not.	67	23	6	3	1	32	53	14

Table 4.6　(continued)

Proposed Change	Would Like Very Much	Would Like	Would Not Like	Would Dislike Very Much	N.A. or Already Have It	Compared to a 2-Hour Reduction in Work Week, This Proposed Change Would Be:		
						More Desir-able	Same	Less Desir-able
5. Having the opportunity to submit written proposals for demonstrations of new or improved ways to deliver services. A committee of social service supervisors, case workers, and administrators would make resources available from a discretionary fund to support the best proposed demonstrations. If you win, you would be in charge of carrying out your own proposal.	42	42	10	2	4	25	42	33
6. Having your working hours reduced by 2 hours a week.	49	33	12	4	2	0	100	0
7. Being allowed to come and go from work at any time you choose—provided you work the same total number of hours each week as you do now. There would be a procedure for coordinating individual schedules.	44	19	20	8	8	19	50	31
8. Being part of a team with your supervisor and coworkers, which would have the authority to decide as a group how the work is done—provided the total output of work is the same as it is now.	39	33	12	3	13	22	49	30
9. Being allowed to take a whole year off with half pay after every 10 years—with no effect on sick leave, annual leave, or terminal leave.	71	15	5	3	6	34	58	8

centages in the last three columns refer only to respondents who answered the questions and who did not indicate that this was something they already had.

Tables 4.3 through 4.6 show that most people in this sample expressed no more desire for a two-hour reduction in their working week than for the other proposed changes, including those which would give them more opportunities for learning and for involvement in the job. While more than half of the whole sample did say they would like very much to have their working hours reduced by two hours a week, the majority of individuals in each occupational group viewed all of the other changes, with one exception, at least as favorably as having this extra time off. (The exception was that most nurse's aides did not prefer having flexible daily hours. This reflects their fear of further disruption in daily work schedules, which are already hard for them to predict or control due to frequent sudden changes.)

It may seem surprising that respondents do not express greater favor for reduction in hours of work. But this finding is consistent with the responses to another question: "Suppose that you won a million dollars in a lottery, and on the same day the city announced it could no longer pay your salary. Would you continue to spend any time at your present job as a volunteer?" Between 25 and 30 percent of the accountants, social service supervisors, and college office assistants answered "yes." And among nurse's aides, who at the time were earning only about $8,000 a year, the proportion who indicated willingness to volunteer was an amazing 77 percent.

These are still only hypothetical expressions of commitment. But we also had one measure of actual commitment. The questionnaire was voluntary and anonymous. At the end was a question asking how long it took to complete it. The average was about 20 minutes. This means that respondents donated a total of about 300 hours of their own time to answering our questions about their work. Even though only a minority of public employees may care this much, the evidence is that some real commitment does exist, with sometimes surprising intensity.

The Problem of Incentives

Unfortunately, according to the people we surveyed there appears to be little if any support for this kind of intrinsic motivation in public employment. Table 4.2 shows few are very satisfied with their opportunity to get recognition for their work, or to have an impact on the way things are done. Many complained that their suggestions for improving operations had simply been ignored. This explains the appeal of proposals like the committee to improve work procedures, or the chance to suggest and demonstrate new ideas (Tables 4.3–4.6). These proposals would increase employees' *power* to make government work better (Kanter and Stein, 1980).

Many of the employees we surveyed also complained about the lack of *material* incentive. Pay and opportunity for promotion elicit less expressed satisfaction than most other aspects of the job listed in Table 4.2. Part of the dissatisfaction with promotional opportunity is due to the civil service system, where promotion requires passing a written test. Our respondents frequently complained that the tests did not measure actual performance or competence. Others complained that the test they wanted to take had not been given in a long time, because there were simply no vacant positions higher up the ladder.

The complaint about lack of opportunity for promotion is apparently common in public employment. A collection of surveys by David Sirota Associates compared attitudes among employees and managers in 10 public agencies and 11 private firms. The questions covered perceptions of organizational effectiveness, job satisfaction, quality of supervision, understanding of job requirements, perceived equity of employment situation, and rewards for performance. It was in this last area that the most striking differences appeared between public and private employees. Of all the questions asked, the one that produced the biggest difference was whether an employee agreed with: "The better my performance, the better will be my opportunity for promotion to a better job." While 49 percent of the private-sector employees said this was true, only 30 percent of public employees agreed (National Center for Productivity and Quality of Working Life, February 1978).

But promotion is not the only way to reward an effective employee, and in an organization that is not growing it is not feasible to offer large numbers of promotions. Another way to reward effective performance is a cash bonus, either for an individual or for a whole group. Awards to individuals have sometimes been used in civil service. Awards to groups have appeared more recently. Group bonuses are apt to be more effective than individual bonuses in situations where the work requires collaboration among individuals. Highly motivated individuals can use the group incentive as an argument to enlist the efforts of coworkers. When teamwork is important, it is undesirable to have the envy and divisiveness that individual incentives may foster (see Lawler, 1975).

Experiments with Group Incentive Plans

A number of experiments with group incentives for public employees were conducted in the 1970s. Examples are:

- The 1972 productivity bargain between the city of Tacoma, Washington, and its firefighters' union. The contractual agreement led to implementation of a proposal by the union, which resulted in a redeployment of resources, reduction of the workweek for firefighters, and better fire protection for citizens, with no extra cost to the city. (National Commission on Productivity and Work Quality, March 1975, p. 80)
- The shared-savings plan for Detroit sanitation workers, negotiated with the unions in 1973. In the first year, workers received bonuses between $.08 and $.23 an hour, based on department-wide savings. Cost to the city has decreased with no apparent decline in quality of service, but the motivating effect on workers might have been even greater if the bonus formula had been less complicated. (National Commission on Productivity and Work Quality, March 1975, pp. 82–86)
- The performance incentive plan put in effect by agreement between the City of Orange, California, and the police association, from July 1973 to March 1975. Across-the-board percentage pay raises were tied to percentage decreases in rapes, robberies, burglaries, and auto thefts. The number of these crimes decreased sufficiently in this period for the police to obtain the maximum pay raise possible under the agreement. (Greiner, 1977)

It is not certain that group bonuses will become a standard solution to the problems of how to reward effective performance by public employees. But already the 1980s have seen one agreement for group productivity bonuses on a scale larger than any in the 1970s: for employees of the U.S. Postal Service (*Business Week*, August 3, 1981).

Group performance incentives or productivity bonuses appear to hold some promise for maintaining high commitment among employees in some parts of the public sector. Fire fighting, trash collection, and mail handling all have immediate, tangible, measurable results. It is more difficult, though not impossible, to design valid performance incentives for public school teachers, social workers, or police, the results of whose work is measured in human behavior. Some of the important results—of teaching, for example—may be subtle and far in the future. Or objectives may be in conflict—for example, public social workers may be charged with both helping their clients and at the same time making sure the clients receive no public benefits to which they are not entitled. Incentive plans have to take into account the complexities of the situation wherever they are to apply. However, public employees, unions, and managers have made progress in tackling these problems.

"Making government work better" is an important part of what governments can do to promote full employment and quality of working life. If employees can remain committed and productive even when their jobs are protected by civil service, then it should be possible to maintain motivation and productivity of employees throughout the economy even when the unemployment rate is low. The public sector could be a showcase for demonstrating how to promote productivity and QWL under conditions of very high job security.

Using Public Employment to Advance the State of the Art: Sabbatical Leave as an Example

In addition to adapting techniques from private enterprise to make government work better, new employment strategies can be developed in the public sector for application throughout the economy. The next chapter will describe a general strategy for profit-seeking firms to promote full employment, productivity, and QWL. Part of the general strategy is to avoid destroying an employment relationship that both the employer and the employee want to continue. Prolonging an employment relationship of value to both parties permits greater investment in the relationship, and also protects the investment.

One of the threats to continuity of the relationship is an employee's occasional desire to take some extended time off. The reason might be the birth of a child, other familial responsibility, travel, or simply a desire to take an extended break. If the desired amount of time off is longer than the amount of sick leave or paid vacation to which the employee is entitled, the two main options for the employee are either to quit and live on savings, borrowed money, spouse's income, or whatever—or else to keep working, unwillingly. Quitting would most likely destroy the employment relationship permanently. Reluctantly continuing to work is likely to mean less effective performance, at least temporarily. What would happen if another option were made available for such occasions—some kind of extended paid leave, or sabbatical?

Public Employees Want Sabbaticals

The public sector is a good place to find out. Public employees, especially in civil service, already have a high degree of job security. But they have no way to take an extended break from work except by giving up their jobs entirely. They are locked in. Not surprisingly, when we asked those in our sample if they would like sabbaticals, the answer was strongly affirmative. Of the hypothetical options we presented, the most popular was "Being allowed to take a whole year off with half pay after every 10 years—with no effect on sick leave, annual leave, or terminal leave." In three of the four occupational groups surveyed—the three that are covered by civil service—this option was liked "very much" by more individuals than was any other option. (See Tables 4.3–4.6.)

These groups preferred the sabbatical option to other options which would have given equivalent reductions in work time. In particular, they generally preferred it to a two-hour reduction in the work week, even though both of these options were stated so that the ratio of pay to time worked would be increased by about the same proportion. That is, reducing the work week by two hours without reducing pay would represent about a 5 percent increase in pay per hour worked. And the sabbatical option would pay 10.5 years of salary for 10 years actually worked—also a 5 percent increase in the rate of pay. But more of our respondents preferred the sabbatical.

There could be many reasons why these respondents preferred to take extra time off in the form of a sabbatical rather than a shorter work week. Having a big stretch of time off makes it possible to do things that would not be possible if the time were available only in two-hour segments each week. It also provides a more complete psychological break from the present job. This is appealing to those suffering from boredom or burnout, as some of our respondents were. Desire for a sabbatical may signal a lack of commitment to the present job, but not necessarily. A dedicated but frustrated employee could be especially in need of a break.

The Effect of Sabbaticals on Productivity

Apart from being a boon to employees, what would sabbaticals do to productivity? If we want innovations in public employment to demonstrate how to maintain productivity under conditions of high job security, it is essential to understand how sabbaticals would affect productivity. One possible positive effect would be that employees return refreshed and ready to put more energy into their work. Reports from Xerox Corporation, which allows a few employees each year to take a year's leave with full pay to engage in public-service activities, indicate that some employees do come back "super-charged-up" (*Wall Street Journal*, May 6, 1981). It is also possible that the prospect of a sabbatical a few years in the future would induce some employees, who otherwise would quit, to stay on the job. If equally productive replacements could not readily be found, then keeping the present employees on the job is good for overall productivity.

On the other hand, quit rates may be higher among employees who have taken sabbatical leave. This appears to be true at Xerox. The cost of replacing those who quit has to be charged against the sabbatical plan—unless those who quit after a sabbatical would have quit anyway. This cost to the employer can be reduced by requiring that employees who quit within a certain amount of time after returning from sabbatical must repay all or part of what they were paid while on leave. Existing sabbatical programs for public school teachers incorporate this kind of penalty.

The clearest way to test how sabbaticals would affect quit rates, morale, and productivity would be to make them available on a trial basis and watch what happens. The trial should take place in an organizational unit for which data on productivity are available. The whole trial would last as long as the sabbatical cycle itself—for instance, if everyone were to be eligible every seven years, the complete trial would take that long. Some results should be available after two or three years, though. Ideally, the control group(s) should be other organizational unit(s) performing the same functions as that where the trial takes place. One trial group would be required for each version of the plan that is to be tested.

Financing of Sabbaticals

One critical question about a sabbatical option is how to finance it. There are several possibilities. For employees covered by collective bargaining, a sabbatical option could be written into the contract. Presumably the union would have to concede some other part of the compensation package in order to get it. Individuals might also trade some of their individual compensation for a paid sabbatical. A recent national survey, described in the next chapter, found a large proportion of employees interested in such a deal. An individual could pay for a sabbatical through special payroll deductions, which would accumulate for a few years until they amounted to enough to finance an extended leave. Some unused sick leave might also be converted to sabbatical leave.

Another possibility would be to allow employees to borrow limited amounts of their accrued retirement benefits—in effect, using pension funds to finance some short periods of "retirement" in mid-career. Public employees' pension funds can already lend money for members' home mortgages in some states (for example, California). Lending for their members' personal "self-renewal," as *Work in America* called it, is analogous. The idea of pension-funded sabbaticals is explored further in the next section.

One financing option that is probably *not* feasible, at least not in the present political climate, is new taxes. But new taxes do not seem necessary. Many employees appear willing to finance sabbaticals themselves by foregoing other compensation. And if experiments prove the positive effect of sabbaticals on productivity to be great enough, foregoing other compensation could be unnecessary.

Governments at any level—local, regional, state, or federal—can develop sabbaticals for their own employees. They may proceed slowly, with limited experiments, or they may go right ahead to implement a full-scale program. Either way, they will not only be offering an option many of their employees want, but will also be providing information to help guide the rest of the economy toward full employment, high productivity, and better quality of working life.

Using the Powers of Government to Promote QWL and Productivity in Private Employment

Governments could allow various tax credits for private employers or employees; set standards of QWL to accompany occupational safety and health or fair labor standards; alter "entitlement programs," including Social Security and unemployment insurance, to create new options for employers and employees; legalize new financial instruments; or actively promote QWL and productivity in other ways. Existing policies of selective deregulation and subsidies for capital formation are by no means the only ways to stimulate productivity.

Work-Sharing Unemployment Insurance

Two particular possibilities, neither of which would require any significant additional spending by governments, would provide new options for allocation of time between paid employment and other uses. One is modification of state unemployment insurance laws to allow work-sharing. Instead of laying off some fraction of its employees when business is slow, an employer can have the option of reducing the paid hours of a larger number of employees. For instance, all employees could be reduced from five to four days a week, instead of having one fifth of them laid off completely. The partially laid off employees could collect unemployment insurance benefits in proportion to how much their paid time was cut back. The theory is that employees whose income, including the partial benefit from unemployment insurance, is cut back by a smaller amount will be less likely to seek other employment than if they were fully laid off and had to rely entirely on unemployment insurance. Work-sharing should therefore avoid destruction of some valued employment relationships when business is slow. California created a work-sharing option in 1978 (California Employment Development Department, 1981), and initial results indicate that the new option does have the intended effect.

Sabbaticals

Another option that could prevent some temporary separations from becoming permanent is paid sabbatical leave. While work-sharing unemployment insurance is designed to avoid some of the damage from employers' decisions to reduce employees' work time, paid sabbaticals could prevent similar damage when employees themselves want a temporary separation. As discussed in the preceding pages, one way to finance sabbaticals is to let employees borrow against their own pension-fund assets. The Social Security system, in particular, could provide this option. In limited amounts, payment of Social Security benefits in the form of sabbaticals rather than pensions would actually strengthen the system in the long run. In the year 2010, the first of the huge numbers of people born between 1945 and 1960 will just be reaching age 65, currently the age of retirement. Social Security will then start demanding a bigger share of national income. Exactly how much bigger is hard to say, but the sheer numbers of people claiming retirement benefits will grow enormously. The number of people of working age (16–64) for every person aged 65 or older has been around five since 1960 and will remain so until 2010 (Munnell, 1977, p. 106). But after 2010 the worker/pensioner ratio will drop sharply, from about five to about three. The economic and political conflict between generations is likely to be sharper than in the late 1970s, when Social Security ran into some short-term liquidity problems.

Creating an option for employees to borrow limited amounts against their own pensions would avoid some of the long-term crunch in Social Security. Consider a person born in 1955, around the peak of the baby boom. Assuming survival to age 65 in 2020, and assuming 65 is still the age when retirement benefits can be paid, this person may then join the large numbers claiming benefits. But suppose this person had interrupted a long period of continuous employment at age 40, in 1995, and had taken a ten-month sabbatical. During those ten months, Social Security paid a sabbatical stipend. In 1980 dollars, the value of the stipend was $250 a month. This would be possible if, under Social Security rules in 1995, this employee was already entitled to retire in 2020 with a monthly benefit worth $675 in 1980 dollars. The $675 in 2020 was discounted to $250 in 1995 using an annual discount rate of 4 percent to include both the chance of death and the rate of interest after inflation. The intent of discounting is to make it actuarially equivalent to the Social Security system whether the benefit is paid in 1995 or in 2020. Keep in mind that the entitlement has already been earned by 1995. Social Security will then avoid a monthly claim of $675 (1980 dollars) in 2020 by paying $250 (1980 dollars) a month in 1995. This assumes that the employee repays the ten-month sabbatical stipend simply by giving up the first ten months of retirement benefits.

Employees might prefer other formulas for repaying the sabbatical stipend. A slightly more complicated formula would allow retirement benefits to be paid at the usual age, but would reduce the amount by a certain proportion for each month of sabbatical stipend taken. Employees who have been paid sabbatical stipends could also have the option to repay through extra payroll deductions after returning to work.

Summary

Sabbatical stipends paid by Social Security and work-sharing unemployment insurance are two examples of what governments can do to create new options for employers and employees in the private sector as well as in public employment. These two specific options would help employers and employees avoid ending relationships that they both would prefer to continue. This is part of the strategy some private enterprises have evolved for promoting productivity and QWL. This strategy, as the next chapter explains, is designed to maintain productivity in a high-employment economy. By providing options that are useful in implementing this strategy, governments can help private enterprises that are trying to position themselves to compete in a full-employment economy.

Chapter 5

WHAT PRIVATE ENTERPRISES CAN DO

This concluding chapter describes a strategy for managing human resources in a profit-seeking organization. The purpose of the strategy is to make the enterprise more viable in a full-employment economy. The strategy has three parts: reduce wasteful layoffs, use slack periods to plan improvements in productivity and quality of working life, and reduce wasteful quits. Organizations that can put this strategy into practice are likely to achieve a higher ratio of sales to payroll cost and to improve their competitive position. Hundreds of companies have already adopted one or more of these practices. The more that do, the more quickly it will become possible to sustain full employment.

A Three-Part Strategy for Managing Human Resources

The general strategy can be summarized in a few words. First, when the volume of sales or production declines, try to postpone layoffs. This will reduce the risk of permanently losing people who would be costly to replace. But since it is also costly to keep people on the payroll when there is not enough work to do, the second part of the strategy is to use the slack time to get ready for the next busy period, when sales or production go up again. The preparations can include preventive maintenance, installation of new equipment, and improvement of the physical plant. They can also include figuring out

113

Table 5.1   Hypothetical Effect of New Personnel Strategy on Sales, Payroll, Prices, and Profits

Quarter	Physical Sales Index		Constant-Dollar Payroll		Relative Price Index		Constant-Dollar Sales		Constant-Dollar Cost Other than Payroll		Constant-Dollar Gross Profit	
	Old	New	Old	New	Old	New	Old	New	Old	New	Old	New
1	100	100	40	40	1.00	1.00	100	100	55	55	5	5
2	80	80	34	36	1.00	1.00	80	80	47	47	−1	−3
3	70	70	28	33	0.95	0.95	67	67	43	43	−4	−9
4	80	80	30	34	1.00	1.00	80	80	47	47	3	−1
5	90	90	35	37	1.00	1.00	90	90	51	51	4	2
6	100	100	40	40	1.00	1.00	100	100	55	55	5	5
7	120	120	50	45	1.00	1.00	120	120	63	63	7	12
8	135	150	60	52	1.10	1.00	149	150	69	75	20	23
9	140	160	65	55	1.20	1.10	168	176	71	78	32	43
10	130	150	55	55	1.20	1.10	156	165	67	75	34	35
11	110	130	45	50	1.20	1.10	132	143	59	67	28	26
12	90	110	35	45	1.10	1.00	99	110	51	59	13	6
13	100	120	40	45	1.10	1.00	110	120	55	63	15	12
14	110	130	45	47	1.10	1.00	121	130	59	67	17	16
15	130	150	55	52	1.10	1.00	143	150	67	75	21	23
16	150	180	70	60	1.20	1.00	180	180	75	84	35	36
17	165	200	85	65	1.30	1.10	215	220	80	89	50	66
18	180	215	100	70	1.40	1.20	252	258	84	92	68	96
19	170	205	90	68	1.40	1.20	238	246	81	90	67	88
20	150	185	70	65	1.30	1.10	195	204	75	85	50	54

how to keep delays and mistakes down when volume increases, planning how to train new hires when the time comes, and otherwise improving the group's cognitive capacities. These preparations should pay off by keeping costs down when business picks up again. The third part of the strategy should also pay off then, especially if the upturn coincides with a period of high GNP growth and low unemployment in the economy as a whole. At such times employees become more likely to quit and find work elsewhere. In some cases this may be the best outcome for all concerned. In other cases employees would prefer to stay, and would be costly to replace, but they decide to quit because they want something they do not have in the present job. The third part of the strategy is discovering these wants and trying to accommodate them before regrettable quits occur.

This may seem like plain common sense to some. Others may remain skeptical, especially about how the company avoids going broke while paying people to prepare for the next upswing. Such skepticism is always warranted. It is true that some organizations may not be able to profit by this strategy. But it is also a fact that hundreds of profitable companies of all sizes are putting one or more parts of this strategy to effective use. The following sections describe actual examples.

None of the actual companies practicing this strategy has made public its own internal records of sales, discounts from posted prices, volume of production, payroll and other variable costs, inventories, new equipment outlays, and everything else necessary to measure how much its profits could have been affected by its personnel strategy. But a hypothetical example can show how the strategy as a whole is intended to work.

A Hypothetical Example

Table 5.1 contains five years of quarterly data for two fictitious companies in the same industry. These could instead be two divisions, plants, or other accounting entities in the same or different companies, as long as the two enterprises produce the same kind of goods or services. For instance, they might be two large supermarkets, located far enough away from each other so that a substantial number of shoppers will continue to buy at the closer one even if the prices are somewhat higher, but also near enough so that some shoppers will be drawn to the one where prices are lower.

One of these enterprises has just adopted the personnel strategy described above. The other continues a traditional strategy. Table 5.1 shows what happens over time. The first pair of columns shows the physical quantity of sales achieved with the "old" strategy compared with the "new." The index is assumed to combine physical quantities of different commodities in some appropriate way. What matters here is how the numbers change. Both enterprises face the same pattern of fluctuating demand, reflected in rising and falling physical quantities of merchandise or services sold. As the five-year history begins, demand has just started to fall after a peak. It falls for three quarters, then rises to a new peak in the ninth quarter. A subsequent three-quarter downturn is followed by another expansion to a new peak in quarter 18.

Physical sales start out the same for the two enterprises, but they grow faster under the new personnel strategy. The different effect of the two strategies shows up first in payroll, recorded in the next two columns. Payroll and other monetary amounts are in thousands of constant dollars. Again, what matters here is how the numbers change, not the absolute amounts. The new strategy calls for slower reduction of payroll when demand falls, and use of slack time to plan improvements in productivity and QWL in preparation for the next upturn. As a result, when demand does pick up again in quarter 4, the enterprise with the new strategy is able to expand physical sales with less addition to payroll cost. As physical sales reach a new high in quarter 7, the new strategy is resulting in more physical sales and higher profit.

Faced with rapidly rising payroll costs and disappointing profits, managers following the old strategy raise their relative prices in quarter 8 and again in quarter 9. This boosts profits, but also diverts some customers to the new-strategy enterprise, which now moves ahead for the first time in physical sales. The constant-dollar value of sales in Table 5.1 is simply the physical sales index multiplied by the relative price index. Costs other than payroll, including both fixed costs and costs that vary with physical sales, are also shown. Constant-dollar profits are constant-dollar sales minus the sum of constant-dollar payroll and other costs. At the new peak in quarter 9, the new strategy is yielding more profits with lower relative prices, because a bigger volume of sales has been achieved with a smaller payroll. The payoff from the new strategy would be even bigger if savings were also achieved in costs other than payroll, but in Table 5.1 this is not assumed.

Another cycle of falling and rising demand occurs in quarters 10 through 18. Again the new strategy postpones layoffs, causing lower profits in quarters 11 through 14. But the investment in planning again pays off in lower payroll costs when sales surpass their previous peak level. Payroll costs are lower because bottlenecks have been anticipated and employees' time is used more efficiently. Training problems have also been anticipated, so when new people do have to be hired they can be put to work with less disruption and delay. Also, problems of scheduling, supervision, and other QWL issues have been anticipated or resolved, so fewer experienced employees are quitting when there are other jobs to be had. The result: as demand grows, the new strategy yields higher profits, lower prices than the competition, and a growing market share.

For the new strategy to work, demand must grow. Macro-economic policy must try to keep aggregate demand growing and overall unemployment down, as Chapter 3 explained. At the same time, the more companies use this kind of strategy for managing human resources, the more feasible such a macroeconomic policy becomes, because it results in less inflation. This personnel strategy is best adapted to a high-demand, high-employment economy. If such conditions do not exist, there is no incentive to adapt to them!

Postponing Layoffs

WE WILL TRY TO MAINTAIN A STABLE WORK FORCE: *Every tactic possible will be employed in order to effectively manage inventory and staffing requirements recognizing that individual needs for job continuity and personal security have impact on attitudes and job performance.*

So states the written "Organizational Philosophy" of an actual plant opened in 1979 to manufacture nutritional products. The new plant opened as the parent corporation's sales were expanding from $272 million in fiscal 1978 to $411 million in fiscal 1980. With its 250 employees all on salary, the plant is an example of what Richard Walton called a "high commitment work system": It both requires and reinforces high commitment on the part of employees. Teams of employees are given as much responsibility as possible for "plan, do, and control." The pay system rewards both team performance and individual acquisition of skills. Individual employees may keep increasing their salaries by formally mastering additional "skill blocks."

Toward that end, each employee is encouraged to outline a "career path." This whole system is designed to achieve continuing growth in productivity with a stable work force. Thus the written commitment to providing as much job security as possible in case of fluctuating demand.

It may be easier to keep such promises in a brand-new facility designed especially for a high-commitment personnel strategy. But there are other examples of companies moving toward no-layoff policies. Control Data Corporation was reported to be implementing such a plan in 1981 for its 57,000 full-time employees. One important consideration for CDC is the high cost of turnover.

It costs an average of $60,000 to hire, move, and train a typical computer programmer. Thus it makes sense to hang on to temporarily surplus employees in a downturn and to handle workload peaks with extensive use of part-time workers, overtime, and subcontracting. Business Week, April 20, 1981, p. 36)

As at the new plant making nutritional products, a no-layoff policy at CDC is seen as consistent with the expectation that employees will keep improving their skills. "We're asking our employees to develop themselves for the company's benefits," according to CDC Deputy Chairman Norbert R. Berg. "That's much easier to ask if the employee knows we expect him to be around for a career."

Delta Airlines is another example of a company trying to minimize layoffs. When the air traffic controllers went on strike in the summer of 1981, forcing a reduction in the number of flights, other airlines laid off thousands of employees. But Delta minimized layoffs by assigning flight crews to jobs on the ground. This was a reflection of Delta's long-term, high-commitment personnel strategy, which has helped it remain profitable while other U.S. airlines have had serious problems (*Business Week*, August 31, 1981).

In California, a total of 1,275 firms—most with 50 employees or less—were reported to have used the work-sharing option in the state's unemployment insurance law. This total is for the 28 months after July 1978, when the work-sharing option became available (see Chapter 4). Work-sharing does not postpone or eliminate layoffs; it only redistributes the reduction in work time among employees. For example, instead of laying off 20 percent of the work force, the work-sharing option allows an employer to keep everyone on the payroll four days a week instead of the regular five. Each employee would then collect unemployment insurance benefits for the day he or she did not work. Although the employer's short-run payroll is reduced by about the same amount, the work-sharing option may prevent the loss of valued employees. This was by far the most frequently cited reason for employers to use the work-sharing option, according to a survey by the California Employment Development Department.

The big difference between work-sharing and actually postponing layoffs is that work-sharing does not necessarily imply bigger current payroll costs to the employer than a standard layoff policy—but postponing layoffs does. The hypothetical numbers in Table 5.1 give an idea of how postponing layoffs can eat up a company's cash flow. This strategy becomes much more practical if the immediate cost can be financed in some way. The possibility of government financing was mentioned in Chapter 4. But what about a company financing this policy itself?

Company Financing of Postponed Layoffs

If a company has profit-sharing, a Scanlon plan, or some other mechanism for paying employees additional money when profit or productivity improves, it is possible to tap into these funds to finance the cost of postponing layoffs. Instead of immediately paying out the full amount of bonus to which employees are entitled under the existing plan, some fraction of the employees' share could be kept in reserve. Then if a drop in demand occurs and some employees become redundant, they can be kept on the payroll and paid out of the accumulated reserve in the productivity bonus fund. While on the payroll, they would spend some time planning and preparing for more efficient operation when demand recovers. If the drop in demand is so steep or so prolonged that outright layoffs are necessary, any funds remaining in the productivity bonus reserve can be paid as supplemental unemployment benefits. These could be paid whether layoffs are distributed in the usual way or by work-sharing. The point is to reserve some of the productivity bonus to postpone layoffs as long as possible, and then to supplement unemployment insurance benefits when postponing layoffs is no longer useful. In addition to enhancing job security, this arrangement would also have a tax advantage for employees: Because the income tax is progressive, bonus payments would be taxed at a higher rate if paid on top of regular earnings, but not if used to maintain earnings at the regular level or to supplement unemployment benefits, which are usually only a fraction of regular earnings.

No matter how it is done, if enough employers adopt a policy of postponing layoffs, the immediate effect will be to keep overall unemployment from rising as fast as it otherwise would when aggregate demand diminishes. This in itself will reduce the stress, crime, illness, and death that unemployment causes. Keeping overall unemployment down also makes it more advantageous for employers to invest, or to continue investing, in improved QWL and more intrinsically motivating work.

Involving Employees in Planning for Productivity

Participation by employees in making decisions about their work has been practiced in countless ways, and advocated in almost as many. Participatory management and organizational development, industrial democracy and sociotechnical systems, McGregor's Theory Y and Likert's System 4, Scanlon plans, quality circles, and QWL programs all prescribe participation. Important differences exist among these approaches in theory, and among the various applications of any one theory in practice (for example, see Williams; also Katzell and Yankelovich).

Almost all applications of these and similar theories have at least one element in common: *meetings*. Participation implies face-to-face meetings of employees. Whether meetings of employees lead to improvements in productivity depends on a host of variables, not the least of which is whether improving productivity is the explicit purpose of the meetings. Empirical studies of the effects of employees' participation never can measure all the relevant variables. One study that did have an unusual amount of data available was reported by Rosenberg and Rosenstein. They analyzed the minutes of 262 meetings of employees in a medium-sized, unionized foundry in the United States. The meetings, held "to discuss means of improving productivity," took place over a period of six years. Data on productivity were also available. The analysis found productivity tended to be higher in periods when meetings were more frequent, when more relevant subjects were discussed, and when a larger proportion of production workers participated. This does not prove that the meetings were responsible for changes in productivity: the reverse may have been true, or something else may have caused both the meetings and productivity to change over time. But this is about as precise as the empirical studies get.

Another study with relatively complete data was published by Espinosa and Zimbalist. They evaluated the program of workers' participation under the short-lived Allende regime in Chile in the early 1970s. Among their conclusions from a comparison of 35 firms was that "higher levels of participation were clearly correlated with greater increases in productivity" (p. 185).

For the most part, quantitative evidence on the effects of employees' participation on productivity in U.S. companies is not published. Companies with formal mechanisms for sharing the gains from increased productivity—for example, Scanlon plans—presumably do collect such evidence, but they have good reason not to allow publication of data that could be useful to their competitors.

Still, the very fact that Scanlon plans and similar schemes continue to be used is evidence that they can work. Eventually, the same may be said about "quality circles" or "quality control circles." These have now been adopted by more than 400 American firms, according to one estimate (Cole, 1981). This boom has been stimulated by competition with the Japanese, who imported the concept of quality circles from the United States and apparently put it to good use. Whether this particular format for participation will now boost U.S. productivity remains to be seen, but many managers evidently find reason to believe it can.

Productivity and Employees' Participation in QWL Programs

A belief that participation raises productivity also underlies efforts to improve QWL in many companies. QWL is a very diffuse notion, with different specific meanings in different places. Chapter 3 defined QWL to include whatever conditions are necessary in a particular organization to motivate employees to give their work more than the minimum of care and effort. In practice, a good deal of the recent activity conducted under the label of QWL has consisted of employees meeting to improve productivity.

General Motors, for example, has been promoting QWL, and has even formed a joint committee with the UAW to oversee QWL efforts. One of GM's showcase plants is in North Tarrytown, New York. The QWL program there has been credited with helping to transform the plant from a disaster to an exemplar over a ten-year period. Two specific illustrations show how QWL promotes participation and productivity:

*Body-shop employees met in a series of "rap sessions" to find so-
lutions for welding problems. Within several months the number of
weld discrepancies was reduced from 35% to 1½% of all welds.*

*Employees of the metal finish department worked with employees
of the paint shop to develop different finishing procedures. As a result,
there was a dramatic drop in the number of metal-finish problems.*
(Walfish, 1977, p. 133)

GM has printed its own booklet, "Quality of Work Life: What's in
a Name?" It was written by Ted Mills, Director of the American
Center for the Quality of Work Life. Mills emphasizes that QWL is
"not a productivity gimmick." It achieves higher productivity, he
insists, by addressing the needs of employees *before* the company's
needs. But his summary of QWL's purpose is

*to provide people at work (managers, supervisors, rank and file
workers) with structured opportunities to become actively involved
in a new interpersonal process of problem-solving toward both a
better way of working and a more effective work organization, the
payoff from which includes the best interests of employees and
employers in equal measure.* (p. 23)

Other examples of companies successfully involving employees in
planning for productivity have been assembled by Edward Glaser.
Among the companies where employees' ideas turned into clear-cut
gains in productivity are Procter and Gamble, the Cryovac Division
of W. R. Grace, and Corning Glass.

Benefits to the Whole Economy

The benefits of providing more scope for responsible employees
have been noted by the financial community. New York Stock Exchange Chairman William H. Batten strongly endorsed QWL as a
means to revive productivity growth. Without departing from the
standard Wall Street theory that "savings and investment is the
single most important element in determining productivity," Batten
nevertheless affirmed with Alfred Marshall that "the most important
of all capital is that invested in human beings." He went on to assert,

*Perhaps the biggest problem today is to reorganize work in ways
that will enable workers to derive satisfaction from it.*

*I believe the best prospects for overcoming the problems I've
been describing are offered by what has come to be known as the
quality-of-work-life movement.*

*The core of this approach is to encourage employees to partici-
pate in the key decisions that affect and determine day-to-day pat-*

terns. It recognizes that the person who does the job is the person who knows the job best. And it seeks to draw upon the expertise and creativity of a better-educated work force to help redesign and reorganize work in ways that meet the needs and demands of working people today and encourage them to maximize their contributions to the productivity of the organizations that employ them.

If the proper work environment is created, the long-term payoff will be productivity improvement through better interpersonal relationships, stronger employee job interest and satisfaction, less absenteeism and waste, and a more useful flow of ideas about how to improve operations. (p. 63)

The more employers can elicit this kind of contribution, the healthier the economy as a whole will be—especially if participating employees can anticipate problems that arise during a prolonged expansion. Avoiding bottlenecks, breakdowns, shortages, and foulups when the economy is operating near capacity will reduce the late-expansion drag on productivity growth (see Chapter 2). Maintaining productivity growth reduces upward pressure on cost and delays the time when either employers themselves have to reduce employment in order to conserve cash, or the government has to reduce overall output and employment in order to suppress rising prices. This is how involving employees in planning for continued productivity growth can help sustain full employment in the economy as a whole.

Avoiding Regrettable Quits

For the individual employer, the point of the whole strategy described here is to gain a competitive edge when business is expanding. That is when having postponed layoffs and having used some slack time for productivity planning should pay off.

Some of the ideas suggested in employees' meetings are directly useful in improving productivity. Other ideas have more to do with improving employees' own comfort, safety, convenience, or general well-being. Improving the general well-being of an employee or group of employees does not necessarily increase the amount they produce, but it may deter them from leaving for other jobs when they have a chance. Alternative job opportunities are most abundant when the economy as a whole is operating at a high level of output and employment. This is when quit rates are highest. When experienced employees quit, there is a negative effect on productivity because the employees who replace them are apt to be less productive, at least initially. Rising quit rates are one reason why overall productivity growth eventually diminishes during a prolonged expansion. Part of the strategy for improving a company's competitive position in a full-employment economy is therefore to deter employees from quitting by accommodating their personal wants where possible.

Flexible Scheduling: A Low-Cost Benefit

Some of these wants can be accommodated at little or no cost. Since every work setting and every employee is unique, there is no way to catalogue all the possible ways in which employees' attachment to their jobs may be strengthened. But some possibilities for making employees' lives easier, at little or no cost to employers, have been demonstrated in a variety of different workplaces. A good example is flexible scheduling. In 1980 more than 7.6 million full-time, nonagricultural employees reported that they were on "flexitime," defined as

> a work schedule that provides individual workers with limited options over the time their workday begins and ends, without affecting their total hours of work over a given period. Details of flexitime differ from one worksite to another, depending on production or customer requirements, public laws, and collective bargaining agreements and other factors. For example, at some sites, the period of time during which workers can arrive (or depart) is half an hour or less; in others, it is 2 hours or more. Some flexitime schedules permit a mix of shorter and longer days, others require workdays of equal length. Again, the period over which total hours of work must equal contractual hours ranges from one day to a month. (U.S. Bureau of Labor Statistics news release, Feb. 24, 1981)

Flexitime allows individual employees to adjust their hours for their own convenience. For example, it allows a person to go to the dentist without having to use short-term sick leave. It also reduces anxiety about getting to work late because of rush-hour traffic or other delays. A review of several dozen case studies and surveys found flexitime was often reported to have improved employees' morale and productivity—though this is not the primary purpose—and at little or no cost to employers. Significantly, "turnover was also reduced in perhaps a third to a half of the cases" (Nollen, 1979, p. 3).

More Expensive Ways to Avoid Quits

Providing individual employees with some choice about hours of work is one way to improve QWL and reduce quits at little or no cost, and it is not surprising that more employers are instituting some form of flexitime. Not all employees' wants can be accommodated at no cost, however. Among the myriad possible improvements that cost money, it is useful to distinguish between those for which the cost can be allocated to individual employees, and those for which the cost is incurred on behalf of a whole group.

Improvements for whole groups include divisible benefits that management decides to provide for everyone—for example, across-the-board increases in pay or other compensation. They also include expenditures for amenities or improved conditions at the work site. For instance, in California's "Silicon Valley," rapid growth in demand for microprocessors in the 1970s created a full-employment economy in microcosm. With employment opportunities so abundant, companies had to make special efforts to hold on to their employees. Some of these efforts included fancy recreational facilities and Friday afternoon "beer blasts."

Expenditures on behalf of whole groups may not be the most cost-effective way to avoid quits, however. Someone who does not swim, play tennis, or drink beer would prefer to have a pay raise than to have the company spend the money on a swimming pool, tennis courts, and beer. But providing across-the-board pay raises big enough to deter quits can be very expensive. This is an argument for seeking improvements that can be offered as options to individual employees.

Reduced-Time Options: Costs Shared by Individuals Who Benefit

Reduced-time options are an example. Some employees are unable or unwilling to work a full day, week, or month. Some do but say they would rather not: Eleven out of every hundred employees in 1978 expressed a general preference for working fewer hours and earning correspondingly less pay (Best, 1980, p. 61). This was discovered in a national survey by the Louis Harris organization for the U.S. Department of Labor and the National Commission on Employment Policy. These employees would have reason to quit their present jobs if they found other employers who could accommodate their preference. But these quits are avoidable if their present employers can find a way to let individuals work part time for partial pay.

The proportion of employees who express a desire for reduced time and correspondingly reduced pay is larger when the option is spelled out in specific terms. The 1978 survey asked each employee

> *How much of your current earnings would you be willing to exchange for various forms of free time. . . . [A]ssume that you are now working about 40 hours a week and that reductions of your work time will not affect your job security.* (Best, 1980, p. 149)

Table 5.2 shows the specific options and the pattern of responses. Each option would cost the employee a proportion of current pay, equal to the proportion by which work time would be reduced. The table shows that about one out of four respondents would like to have a shorter work day or week, along with a proportionate reduction in pay. Interestingly, more than five out of every dozen employees (42 percent) say they would accept small reductions in pay in return for more paid vacation days every year, or for a paid sabbatical every seventh year.

Even larger numbers of employees say they would like reduced-time options if they could get them by surrendering some or all of a pay *increase*, rather than part of their *current* pay. Table 5.3 shows the specific options and responses. Now almost *two out of three* employees say they would trade some pay for additional paid vacation days every year or a paid sabbatical every seventh year.

The apparent interest in these options in a national survey suggests that more companies could give themselves an edge in recruiting and retaining employees by making reduced-time options more available. In some situations some of these options are not feasible due to staffing requirements, shift schedules, union contracts, or other reasons. Where they are feasible, and where there is an expressed interest among the company's own employees, reduced-time options could be a cost-effective way to reduce turnover. The cost advantage to employers is in the simple fact that employees who use these options absorb the cost themselves.

The most conventional form of reduced-time option is regular part-time work. As of 1979 there were 12.2 million employees who voluntarily worked part-day or part-week schedules. Regular part-time workers were about 14 percent of all nonagricultural employees in 1979. From 1969 to 1979 the number of part-timers grew 35 percent, while the number of full-timers grew 23 percent. About 41

Table 5.2 Stated Worker Preferences Toward Exchanging Portions of Current Income for Alternative Forms of Free Time (percentage breakdown)

Value of Tradeoff	Shorter Workday vs. Pay	Reduced Workweek vs. Pay	Added Vacation vs. Pay	Sabbatical Leave vs. Pay	Earlier Retirement vs. Pay
Nothing for time	77.0	73.8	57.8	57.9	64.0
2% of pay for time	8.7	11.6	23.2	24.4	17.6
5% of pay for time	5.8	—	8.5	8.0	8.1
10% of pay for time	—	7.6	6.2	4.8	5.9
12% of pay for time	5.5	—	—	—	—
15% of pay for time	—	—	—	4.8	—
20% of pay for time	—	4.5	2.2	—	4.4
30% of pay for time	1.6	—	—	—	—
33% of pay for time	—	—	2.0	—	—
40% of pay for time	—	0.9	—	—	—
50% of pay for time	1.5	1.6	—	—	—
Total Percent	100.0	100.0	100.0	100.0	100.0
Total Respondents	954	953	952	951	951

QUESTIONS:

Workday. What is the largest portion of your current yearly income that you would be willing to give up for shorter workdays? (A) Nothing, (B) 2% (1/50th) of your income for 10 minutes off each workday, (C) 5% (1/20th) of your income for 25 minutes off each workday, (D) 12% (1/8th) of your income for 1 hour off each workday, (E) 30% of your income for 2 hours off each workday, (F) 50% (1/2) of your income for 4 hours off each workday.

Workweek. What is the largest portion of your current yearly income that you would be willing to give up for shorter workweeks? (A) Nothing, (B) 2% (1/50th) of your income for 50 minutes off 1 workday a week, (C) 10% (1/10th) of your income for 4 hours off 1 workday a week, (D) 20% (1/5th) of your income for 1 full workday off each week, (E) 40% (4/10ths) of your income for 2 full workdays off each week, (F) 50% (1/2) of your income for 2 full workdays off each week.

Vacation. What is the largest portion of your current yearly income that you would be willing to give up for more paid vacation time? (A) Nothing, (B) 2% (1/50th) of your income for 5 workdays added paid vacation each year, (C) 5% (1/20th) of your income for 12½ workdays added paid vacation each year, (D) 10% (1/10th) of your income for 25 workdays added paid vacation each year, (E) 20% (1/5th) of your income for 50 workdays added paid vacation each year, (F) 33% (1/3rd) of your income for 87½ workdays (17½ workweeks) added paid vacation each year.

Sabbatical. What is the largest portion of your current yearly income that you would be willing to give up in exchange for an extended leave without pay every seventh year? (A) Nothing, (B) 2% (1/50th) of your yearly income for 7 workweeks paid leave after six years of work, (C) 5% (1/20th) of your income for 17½ workweeks paid leave after six years of work, (D) 10% (1/10th) of your income for 35 workweeks paid leave after six years of work, (E) 15% (3/20ths) of your income for 52 workweeks (1 workyear) paid leave after six years of work.

Earlier Retirement. What is the largest portion of your current yearly income that you would be willing to give up in exchange for earlier retirement? (A) Nothing, (B) 2% (1/50th) of your income for earlier retirement at a rate of 5 workdays for every year worked until retirement, (C) 5% (1/20th) of your income for earlier retirement at a rate of 12½ workdays for every year worked until retirement, (D) 10% (1/10th) of your income for earlier retirement at a rate of 25 workdays for every year worked until retirement, (E) 20% (1/5th) of your income for earlier retirement at a rate of 50 workdays for every year worked until retirement.

Note: Column spaces are frequently blank for many tradeoff options because questions dealing with different forms of free time did not always have parallel exchange options.

SOURCE: Best, 1980, p. 81.

Table 5.3   Stated Worker Preferences Toward Exchanging All or Portions of a
Ten-Percent Pay Raise for Alternative Forms of Free Time (percentage breakdown)

Value of Tradeoff	Reduced Workday vs. Raise	Reduced Workweek vs. Raise	Added Vacation vs. Raise	Sabbatical vs. Raise	Earlier Retirement vs. Raise
No part of raise for free time	73.2	56.5	34.4	34.7	48.6
40% of raise for free time	6.7	15.4	31.8	34.2	19.3
70% of raise for free time	4.9	5.3	4.5	8.1	8.3
100% of raise for free time	14.1	22.8	29.4	23.0	23.7
Total Percent	100.0	100.0	100.0	100.0	100.0
Total Respondents	950	952	954	949	952

QUESTIONS:
Workday.   Which one of the following choices between a pay raise and a shorter workday would you select? (A) 10% pay raise and no reduction of the workday, (B) 6% pay raise and a 19-minute reduction of each workday, (C) 3% pay raise and a 34-minute reduction of each workday, (D) no pay raise and a 48-minute reduction of each workday.

Workweek.   Which one of the following choices between a pay raise and a shorter workweek would you select? (A) 10% pay raise and no reduction of each workweek, (B) 6% pay raise and a 1 2/3 hour reduction of each workweek, (C) 3% pay raise and a 2 4/5 hour reduction of each workweek, (D) no pay raise and a 4-hour reduction of each workweek.

Vacation.   Which one of the following choices between a pay raise and a longer paid vacation would you select? (A) 10% pay and no added vacation time, (B) 6% pay raise and 10 workdays of added vacation, (C) 3% pay raise and 17½ workdays added vacation, (D) no pay raise and 25 workdays added vacation.

Sabbatical.   What is your choice between a pay raise and an extended leave with pay from work after six years of work? (A) 10% pay raise and no leave time, (B) 6% pay raise and 12 workweeks (60 workdays) paid leave, (C) 3% pay raise and 21 workweeks (105 workdays) paid leave, (D) no pay raise and 30 workweeks (150 workdays) paid leave.

Earlier Retirement.   What is your choice between a pay raise and earlier retirement? (A) 10% pay raise and no change in retirement plan, (B) 6% pay raise and 10 workdays earlier retirement for each future year of work, (C) 3% pay raise and 17½ workdays earlier retirement for each future year of work, (D) no pay raise and 25 workdays earlier retirement for each future year of work.

SOURCE: Best, 1980, p. 72

percent of part-time employees were married women living with their husbands; this proportion stayed constant over the decade (*Handbook of Labor Statistics 1980*, Table 23).

Sabbaticals as a Reduced-Time Option

The most unconventional of the reduced-time options presented in the 1978 survey is the sabbatical. According to Fred Best, an authority on time-use options who analyzed the survey data,

> *The popularity of the sabbatical is something of a surprise. The concept is hardly known, let alone practiced, outside of academia. Thus, it must appear as rather strange and exotic to the average American. For this reason, it is noteworthy that so many workers stated a willingness to forego income for this type of free time.* (p. 94)

It is also noteworthy that the 1974 survey reported in Chapter 4 (see Tables 4.3–4.6) found similar enthusiasm for sabbaticals. The two surveys corroborate each other.

Since sabbaticals are relatively unconventional, how to pay for them is less obvious. Xerox Corporation simply pays the salaries of the limited number of employees who take public-service leave. But many companies would be reluctant to do this, especially if sabbaticals were to become an option for all employees. The 1978 survey found that many employees themselves would be willing to pay the cost through direct payroll deductions that would accrue over the years. Alternatively, instead of paying in advance, employees could pay for their own sabbaticals by borrowing from their own pension fund accounts. Chapter 4 described the possibility of using Social Security for this purpose. The same argument made there—that allowing employees to use some of their retirement benefits before the usual retirement age would actually protect the Social Security system against a rapid rise in claims after the year 2010—also applies to corporate pension plans. Many corporate pension plans already have unfunded liabilities of alarming size. At General Motors, for example, unfunded pension liabilities in 1981 were 23 percent of the company's net worth (*Business Week*, September 14, 1981, p. 114). When the baby-boom generation starts claiming retirement benefits after the year 2010, even the most prudently managed pension funds are likely to face cash-flow problems. Paying some of these claims before the year 2010 would help avoid such emergencies. But financing sabbaticals out of pension plans is not the only way to pay for them. Payment by employees in advance is also possible, through payroll deductions. And some employers will find it worthwhile to pay all or part of the cost themselves, as Xerox does.

Like the other reduced-time options, sabbaticals are part of the strategy for avoiding regrettable quits. A sabbatical leave is a temporary quit. It is designed to deter permanent quits by allowing an employee to spend time with family or on some project that cannot be accomplished in less than a few weeks or months. The time might be used for pure rest and recreation; even the most dedicated worker may feel the need for an extended vacation every few years. But the essential feature is that the employee and employer be able to reestablish their relationship when the sabbatical is over. To minimize the chance that the temporary quit becomes a permanent separation, it makes sense to use the sabbatical as part of a career-development plan. As more companies engage in formal career planning with their employees, the possibility for constructive use of sabbaticals increases. Among the corporate leaders in career development for employees are IBM, Polaroid, AT&T, Control Data, General Electric, and Citicorp (Cohen, 1981).

Conclusion

Career development, sabbaticals, and flexitime are only examples of the possibilities for improving QWL. This chapter has explained how such improvement can be part of a coherent strategy for maintaining long-term employment relationships and continuing growth in productivity.

Since every organization is different, no two will put this strategy into practice in exactly the same way. And some will not adopt this strategy at all. There are some jobs where automation makes more sense than trying to provide for intrinsic motivation. But the future envisioned in this book is not a fully automated economy where human effort has become unnecessary. Sustaining full employment does not imply an end to scarcity—or an end to growth. If the arguments here are correct, sustained full employment can be achieved by continuation and extension of certain existing practices. Organizations that adopt these practices are building for full employment, and in a fully employed economy they are likely to prosper.

BIBLIOGRAPHY

ALBER, ANTONE F. "Job Enrichment Programs Seen Improving Employee Performance, But Benefits Not Without Cost," *World of Work Report* 3(1):8–11, January 1978.

BAILY, MARTIN N. Comments on paper by Norsworthy, Harper, and Kunze, *Brookings Papers on Economic Activity* 1979 (2), pp. 433–436.

————. "Productivity and the Services of Capital and Labor," *Brookings Papers on Economic Activity* 1981(1), pp. 1–50.

BAILY, MARTIN N., and JAMES TOBIN. "Macroeconomic Effects of Selective Public Employment and Wage Subsidies," *Brookings Papers on Economic Activity* 1977 (2), pp. 511–544.

BALK, WALTER L. (ed.) *Administering State Government Productivity Improvement Programs*. Albany, New York: State University of New York, Graduate School of Public Affairs, 1974(a).

BALK, WALTER L. "Why Don't Public Administrators Take Productivity More Seriously?" *Public Personnel Management* July–August 1974, pp. 318–324(b).

BATTEN, WILLIAM M. "N.Y. Stock Exchange Chairman Cites Role of QWL in Boosting Productivity," *World of Work Report* 5(9):58–63, September 1980.

BERNSTEIN, PAUL. *Workplace Democratization*. Kent, Ohio: Kent State University Press, 1976.

BEST, FRED. *Exchanging Earnings for Leisure: Findings of an Exploratory National Survey on Work Time Preference*, U.S. Department of Labor, R&D Monograph 79. Washington, D.C.: U.S. Government Printing Office, 1980.

BLINDER, ALAN. *Economic Policy and the Great Stagflation*. New York: Academic Press, 1979.

BLUESTONE, IRVING. "Creating a New World of Work," *International Labour Review* 115(1):1–10, January-February, 1977.

————. "Human Dignity Is What It's All About," *Viewpoint* 8(3). Washington, D.C.: Industrial Union Department, AFL-CIO, 1978.

BLUM, ALBERT A., MICHAEL L. MOORE, and B. PARKER FAIREY. "The Effect of Motivational Programs on Collective Bargaining," *Personnel Journal*, July 1973, pp. 633–641.

BODDY, RAFORD, and JAMES CROTTY. "Class Conflict and Macro-Policy: The Political Business Cycle," *The Review of Radical Political Economics* 7(1):1–19, Spring 1975.

BOSWORTH, BARRY. "Re-establishing an Economic Consensus: An Impossible Agenda?" *Daedalus*, Summer 1980, pp. 59–70.

131

BRENNER, HARVEY. "Estimating the Social Costs of National Economic Policy: Implications for Mental and Physical Health, and Criminal Aggression," Paper No. 5 on *Achieving the Goals of the Employment Act of 1946—Thirtieth Anniversary Review*. U.S. Congress, Joint Economic Committee, October 26, 1976.

BURTON, JOHN F., and JOHN E. PARKER. "Inter-Industry Variations in Voluntary Labor Mobility," *Industrial and Labor Relations Review* 22:199–216, January 1969.

Business Week. "Stonewalling Plant Democracy," March 28, 1977.

————. "Where White-Collar Status Boosts Productivity," May 23, 1977, pp. 80–85.

————. "The Pinch on Public Employees," June 23, 1980, pp. 71–77.

————. "The New Industrial Relations," May 11, 1981, pp. 84–98.

————. "A Postal Pact Weighted in Favor of Productivity," August 3, 1981, pp. 26–31.

————. "Pension Liabilities: Improvement Is Illusory," September 14, 1981, pp. 114–118.

CAIN, GLEN G. "The Challenge of Segmented Labor Market Theories to Orthodox Theory: A Survey," *Journal of Economic Literature* 14(4):1215–1267, December 1976.

CALAME, BYRON E. "Wary Labor Eyes Job Enrichment," *Wall Street Journal*, February 26, 1973.

California Employment Development Department. *Interim Evaluation of California Work Sharing Unemployment Insurance Program*. Sacramento, California: California Employment Development Department, 1981.

CARNOY, MARTIN, and DEREK SHEARER. *Economic Democracy, The Challenge of the 1980s*. White Plains, N.Y.: M. E. Sharpe, 1980.

CHICKERING, A. LAWRENCE (ed.). *Public Employee Unions*. San Francisco: Institute for Contemporary Studies, 1976.

COHEN, BARBARA S. "Working with Employees to Assess Skills, Plan the Future," *World of Work Report* 6(8):61–62, August 1981.

COLE, ROBERT E. "QC Warning Voiced by U.S. Expert on Japanese Circles," *World of Work Report* 6(7):49–51, July 1981.

Committee for Economic Development. *Improving Productivity in State and Local Government*. New York: Committee for Economic Development, March 1976.

DAVIS, LOUIS E., and JAMES C. TAYLOR (eds.). *Design of Jobs*. Middlesex, England: Penguin Books, 1972.

DAVIS, LOUIS E., and ERIC L. TRIST: "Improving the Quality of Work Life: Sociotechnical Case Studies," in James O'Toole (ed.), *Work and the Quality of Life*, Resource Papers for *Work in America*. Cambridge, Mass.: MIT Press, 1974.

DAVIS, LOUIS E., ALBERT B. CHERNS and ASSOCIATES. *The Quality of Working Life*, vol. 2, Cases and Commentary. New York: Free Press, 1975.

DENISON, EDWARD F. *Accounting for Slower Economic Growth, the United States in the 1970s*; Washington, D.C.: Brookings Institution, 1979.

————. Comments on paper by Norsworthy, Harper, and Kunze, *Brookings Papers on Economic Activity* 1979(2), pp 436–440.

DEWEY, JOHN. *Democracy and Education: An Introduction to the Philosophy of Education*. New York: Macmillan Co., 1923.

DOUTY, H.M. *Labor-Management Productivity Committees in American Industry*. Washington, D.C.: National Commission on Productivity and Work Quality, May 1975.

DOYLE, ROBERT J. "A New Look at the Scanlon Plan," *Management Accounting*, September 1970.

Economic Report of the President, with the Annual Report of the Council of Economic Advisors. Washington, D.C.: U.S. Government Printing Office, published annually.

ESPINOSA, JUAN G., and ANDREW S. ZIMBALIST. *Economic Democracy, Workers' Participation in Chilean Industry 1970–1973*. New York: Academic Press, 1978.

FAIR, RAY C. *The Short-Run Demand for Workers and Hours*. Amsterdam and London: North-Holland, 1969.

FEIN, MITCHELL. "The Real Needs and Goals of Blue Collar Workers," Conference Board *Record*, February 1973, pp. 26–33.

FELDSTEIN, MARTIN S. "Lowering the Permanent Rate of Unemployment." U.S. Congress, Joint Economic Committee, September 18, 1973.

FLYNN, RALPH J. *Public Work, Public Workers*. Washington, D.C.: New Republic Book Company, 1975.

FORD, ROBERT N. *Motivation Through the Work Itself*. New York: American Management Association, 1969.

FOULKES, FRED K. *Creating More Meaningful Work*. New York: American Management Association, 1969.

FRIEDMAN, MILTON. "The Role of Monetary Policy," *American Economic Review* 58(1):1–17, March 1968.

FRIEDMAN, MILTON and ROSE. *Free to Choose*. New York: Avon, 1981.

FROST, CARL F., JOHN H. WAKELY, and ROBERT A. RUH. *The Scanlon Plan for Organization Development: Identity, Participation, and Equity*. East Lansing, Michigan: Michigan State University Press, 1974.

GINZBERG, ELI. *Good Jobs, Bad Jobs, No Jobs*. Cambridge, Mass.: Harvard University Press, 1979.

GLASER, EDWARD M. *Productivity Gains through Worklife Improvement*. New York: Harcourt Brace Jovanovich, 1976.

GOODMAN, ROBERT K., J. H. WAKELEY, and R. H. RUH. "What Employees Think of the Scanlon Plan," *Personnel*, September-October 1972, pp. 22–29.

GORDON, DAVID M. "Capital-Labor Conflict and the Productivity Slowdown," *American Economic Review* 71(2):30–35, May 1981.

GORDON, ROBERT AARON. *The Goal of Full Employment*. New York: Wiley, 1967.

GORDON, ROBERT J. "The 'End-of-Expansion' Phenomenon in Short-Run Productivity Behavior," *Brookings Papers on Economic Activity* 1979(2), pp. 447–461.

GREENBLATT, ALAN. "Maximizing Productivity through Job Enrichment," *Personnel*, March-April 1973.

GREINER, JOHN M., ROGER E. DAHL, HARRY P. HATRY, and ANNIE P. MILLAR. *Monetary Incentives and Work Standards in Five Cities: Impacts and Implications for Management and Labor*. Washington, D.C.: Urban Institute, 1977.

HACKMAN, J. RICHARD. "On the Coming Demise of Job Enrichment," in E. L. Cass and F. G. Zimmer (eds.), *Man and Work in Society*. New York: Van Nostrand Reinhold, 1975.

————. *Improving the Quality of Work Life: Work Design*, monograph prepared for the U.S. Department of Labor (Contract No. L-74-77). Washington, D.C.: U.S. Department of Labor, June 1975.

HALL, ROBERT E. "Employment Fluctuations and Wage Rigidity," *Brookings Papers on Economic Activity* 1980(1), pp. 91–123.

HENLE, PETER. "Economic Effects: Reviewing the Evidence," in Jerome M. Rosow (ed.), *The Worker and the Job, Coping with Change*. New York: The American Assembly, Columbia University, 1974.

HERZBERG, FREDERICK. "One More Time: How Do You Motivate Employees?" *Harvard Business Review* 46(1):53–62, 1968.

HERZBERG, FREDERICK, BERNARD MAUSNER, and BARBARA SNYDERMAN. *The Motivation to Work* (2nd ed.). New York: Wiley, 1959.

HOERR, JOHN. "Worker Unrest: Not Dead, but Playing Possum," *Business Week*, May 10, 1976.

HULTGREN, THOR. *Cost, Prices, and Profits: Their Cyclical Relations*. New York: National Bureau of Economic Research, distributed by Columbia University Press, 1965.

HUNNIUS, GERRY, G. DAVID GARSON, and JOHN CASE (eds.). *Workers' Control*. New York: Random House (Vintage Books), 1973.

IMAN, STEPHEN C. "The Development of Participation by Semiautonomous Work Teams: The Case of Donnelly Mirrors," in Davis and Cherns, 1975, pp. 216–231.

International City Management Association. *Public Management* 56(6), June 1974 (entire issue on productivity improvement).

JAQUES, ELLIOTT. *Measurement of Responsibility*. Cambridge, Mass.: Harvard University Press, 1956.

JENKINS, DAVID J. *Job Power*. Garden City, N.Y.: Doubleday, 1973.

KANTER, ROSABETH MOSS, and BARRY A. STEIN. "Value Change and the Public Sector Work Force: Labor Force Trends, the Salience of Opportunity and Power, and Implications for Public Sector Management," in *The Changing Character of the Public Work Force*. Washington, D.C.: Office of Personnel Management, 1980.

KATZELL, RAYMOND A., DANIEL YANKELOVICH, et al. *Work, Productivity, and Job Satisfaction*. New York: Harcourt Brace Jovanovich, 1975.

KENDRICK, JOHN W. "Productivity Trends and Prospects," in U.S. Congress, Joint Economic Committee, *U.S. Economic Growth from 1976 to 1986: Prospects, Problems, and Patterns*, Volume I—Productivity. Washington, D.C.: U.S. Government Printing Office, October 1, 1976, pp. 1–20.

KENDRICK, JOHN W., and ELLIOT S. GROSSMAN. *Productivity in the United States, Trends and Cycles*. Baltimore, Md.: Johns Hopkins University Press, 1980.

KENISTON, KENNETH, and the Carnegie Council on Children. *All Our Children*. New York: Harcourt Brace Jovanovich, 1977.

KETCHUM, LYMAN D. "A Case Study of Diffusion," in Davis and Cherns, 1975, pp. 138–163.

KOVACH, KENNETH A. "State and Local Public Employee Labor Relations—Where Are They Headed?" *Journal of Collective Negotiations in the Public Sector* 8(1):19–30, 1979.

KRAFT, W. PHILIP, and KATHLEEN L. WILLIAMS. "Job Redesign Improves Productivity," *Personnel Journal*, July 1975.

LAWLER, EDWARD E. *Improving the Quality of Work Life: Reward Systems*, prepared for U.S. Department of Labor, Contract No. L-74-78. Ann Arbor, Michigan: University of Michigan, June 1975 (typescript).

LAZEAR, EDWARD P. "Agency, Earnings Profiles, Productivity, and Hours Restrictions," *American Economic Review* 71(4):606–620, September 1981.

LIGHT, RICHARD J. "Abused and Neglected Children in America: A Study of Alternative Policies," *Harvard Educational Review* 43(4):556–598, November 1973.

LOFTUS, JOSEPH A., and BEATRICE WALFISH. *Breakthroughs in Union-Management Cooperation*. Scarsdale, N.Y.: Work in America Institute, 1977.

LUCAS, ROBERT E., JR. "Expectations and the Neutrality of Money," *Journal of Economic Theory* 4(2):103–124, April 1972.

————. "Tobin and Monetarism: A Review Article"; *Journal of Economic Literature* 19:558–567, June 1981.

LUCAS, ROBERT E. B. "Hedonic Wage Equations and Psychic Wages in the Returns to Schooling," *American Economic Review* 67(4):549–558, September 1977.

MACCOBY, MICHAEL. "Changing Work: The Bolivar Project," *Working Papers* 3:43–55, Summer 1975.

MAHER, JOHN R. (ed.). *New Perspectives in Job Enrichment*. New York: Van Nostrand Reinhold, 1971.

McCONNELL, CAMPBELL R. "Why Is U.S. Productivity Slowing Down?" *Harvard Business Review*, March-April 1979, pp. 36–44, 48–56.

MILLER, G. WILLIAM. "The Role of Productivity Gains in Solving National Economic Problems," remarks before the American Productivity Center, New York City, October 3, 1978.

MILLS, TED. "Quality of Work Life: What's in a Name?" General Motors Corp., 1978.

MOORE, BRIAN E., and TIMOTHY L. ROSS. *The Scanlon Way to Improved Productivity: A Practical Guide*. New York: Wiley, 1978.

MUNNELL, ALICIA H. *The Future of Social Security*. Washington, D.C.: Brookings Institution, 1977.

National Center for Productivity and Quality of Working Life. *Labor-Management Committees in the Public Sector, Experiences of Eight Committees*. Washington, D.C.: National Center for Productivity and Quality of Working Life, November 1975.

————. *Recent Initiatives in Labor-Management Cooperation*. Washington, D.C.: National Center for Productivity and Quality of Working Life, February 1976.

————. *Improving Governmental Productivity: Selected Case Studies*. Washington, D.C.: National Center for Productivity and Quality of Working Life, Spring 1977.

————. *Productivity and Job Security: Retraining to Adapt to Technological Change*. Washington, D.C.: National Center for Productivity and Quality of Working Life, Winter 1977.

————. *Employee Attitudes and Productivity Differences Between the Public and*

Private Sector. Washington, D.C.: National Center for Productivity and Quality of Working Life, Fall 1978.

————. *Directory of Productivity and Quality of Working Life Centers*. Washington, D.C.: National Center for Productivity and Quality of Working Life, Fall 1978.

National Commission on Productivity. *Second Annual Report*. Washington, D.C.: U.S. Government Printing Office, March 1973.

National Commission on Productivity and Work Quality. *Employee Incentives to Improve State and Local Government Productivity*. Washington, D.C.: National Commission on Productivity and Work Quality, March 1975.

NEWLAND, CHESTER A. (ed.) "Symposium: Productivity in Government," *Public Administration Review* 32(6):739–850, November/December 1972.

NOLLEN, STANLEY. *New Patterns of Work*. Scarsdale, N.Y.: Work in America Institute, 1979.

NORSWORTHY, J.R., MICHAEL J. HARPER, and KENT KUNZE. "The Slowdown in Productivity Growth: Analysis of Some Contributing Factors," *Brookings Papers on Economic Activity* 1979(2), pp. 387–421.

OKUN, ARTHUR M., and GEORGE L. PERRY (eds.). *Curing Chronic Inflation*. Washington, D.C.: Brookings Institution, 1978.

OKUN, ARTHUR M. *Prices and Quantities: A Macroeconomic Analysis*. Washington, D.C.: Brookings Institution, 1981.

OSTER, GERRY. "Labor Relations and Demand Relations: A Case Study of the Unemployment Effect," *Cambridge Journal of Economics* 4(4):337–348, December 1980.

O'TOOLE, JAMES, et al. *Work in America*. Cambridge, Mass.: MIT Press, 1973.

O'TOOLE, JAMES. *Work, Learning, and the American Future*. San Francisco: Jossey-Bass, 1977.

PARNES, STEVEN. *Productivity and the Quality of Working Life, Highlights of the Literature*. Scarsdale, N.Y.: Work in America Institute, 1978.

PAUL, WILLIAM J., JR., KEITH B. ROBERTSON, and FREDERICK HERZBERG. "Job Enrichment Pays Off," *Harvard Business Review*, March-April, 1969.

PECHMAN, JOSEPH A. (ed.) *Setting National Priorities, the 1978 Budget*. Washington, D.C.: Brookings Institution, 1977.

————. *Setting National Priorities, The 1979 Budget*. Washington, D.C.: Brookings Institution, 1978.

————. *Setting National Priorities, The 1980 Budget*. Washington, D.C.: Brookings Institution, 1979.

PERRY, GEORGE L. "Labor Force Structure, Potential Output, and Productivity," *Brookings Papers on Economic Activity* 1971, no. 3, pp. 533–565.

PHELPS, EDMUND S. "Money-Wage Dynamics and Labor-Market Equilibrium," *Journal of Political Economy* 76(4):678–711, July/August 1968.

QUINN, ROBERT P., and LINDA J. SHEPARD. *The 1972–73 Quality of Employment Survey*. Ann Arbor, Michigan: Survey Research Center, University of Michigan, 1974.

QUINN, ROBERT P., and GRAHAM L. STAINES. *The 1977 Quality of Employment Survey*. Ann Arbor, Michigan: Institute for Social Research, University of Michigan, 1979.

ROBERTS, KARLENE H., and WILLIAM GLICK. "The Job Characteristics Approach to Task Design: A Critical Review." Berkeley, Calif.: School of Business Administration, University of California (typescript, no date).

ROSENBERG, RICHARD D., and ELIEZER ROSENSTEIN. "Participation and Productivity: An Empirical Study," *Industrial and Labor Relations Review* 33(3):355–367, April 1980.

ROSS, HEATHER L., and ISABEL V. SAWHILL. *Time of Transition, The Growth of Families Headed by Women*. Washington, D.C.: Urban Institute, 1975.

RUSH, HAROLD. *Job Design for Motivation*. New York: The Conference Board, 1971.

———. *Organization Development: A Reconnaissance*. New York: The Conference Board, 1973.

RUSSELL, RAYMOND, ART HOCHNER, and STEWART E. PERRY. "San Francisco's 'Scavengers' Run Their Own Firms," *Working Papers for a New Society* 5(2):30–37, Summer 1977.

SARGENT, THOMAS J. "The Observational Equivalence of Natural and Unnatural Rate Theories of Macroeconomics," *Journal of Political Economy* 84(3):631–640, 1976.

———. *Macroeconomic Theory*. New York: Academic Press, 1979.

SHEPPARD, HAROLD L., and NEAL Q. HERRICK. *Where Have All the Robots Gone?* New York: Free Press, 1972.

SIMS, CHRISTOPHER A. "Output and Labor Input in Manufacturing," *Brookings Papers on Economic Activity* 1974(3), pp. 695–735.

SMITH, ADAM. *The Wealth of Nations*. New York: Random House, 1937.

SMITH, ROBERT S. "Compensating Wage Differentials and Public Policy: A Review," *Industrial and Labor Relations Review* 32(3):339–352, April 1979.

STAINES, GRAHAM L. "Is Worker Dissatisfaction Rising?" *Challenge* 22(2):38–45, May/June 1979.

STERN, DAVID. "Willingness to Pay for More Agreeable Work," *Industrial Relations* 17(1):85–90, February 1978.

STERN, DAVID, and DANIEL FRIEDMAN. "Short-Run Behavior of Labor Productivity: Tests of the Motivation Hypothesis," *Journal of Behavioral Economics* 9(2):89–105, Winter 1980.

STOIKOV, VLADIMIR, and ROBERT L. RAIMON. "Determinants of Differences in the Quit Rate Among Industries," *American Economic Review* 58:1283–1298, December 1968.

STRAUSS, GEORGE. "Job Satisfaction, Motivation, and Job Redesign," in George Strauss, Raymond E. Miles, Charles C. Snow, and Arnold S. Tannenbaum (eds.), *Organizational Behavior, Research and Issues*. Madison, Wisconsin: Industrial Relations Research Association, 1974.

THUROW, LESTER. *Generating Inequality*. New York: Basic Books, 1975.

TOBIN, JAMES. "Stabilization Policy Ten Years After," *Brookings Papers on Economic Activity* 1980(1), pp. 19–71.

U.S. Congress. *Employment Act of 1946*, P.L. 79-304, February 20, 1946.

———. *Full Employment and Balanced Growth Act of 1978*, P.L. 95-523, October 27, 1978.

U.S. Congress, Congressional Budget Office. *The Productivity Problem: Alternatives for Action*. Washington, D.C.: U.S. Government Printing Office, 1981.

U.S. Department of Labor, Bureau of Labor Statistics. "Labor Turnover in Manufacturing," Bulletin 76-1364. Washington, D.C.: Bureau of Labor Statistics, October 29, 1976.

————. "The Manufacturing Quit Rate: Trends, Cycles, and Interindustry Variations," BLS Staff Paper 7. Washington, D.C.: Bureau of Labor Statistics, 1973.

————. *Handbook of Labor Statistics 1975—Reference Edition*, Bulletin 1865. Washington, D.C.: U.S. Government Printing Office, 1975.

————. *Handbook of Labor Statistics 1977*, Bulletin 1966. Washington, D.C.: U.S. Government Printing Office, 1977.

————. *Handbook of Labor Statistics 1980*, Bulletin 2070. Washington, D.C.: U.S. Government Printing Office, 1980.

U.S. House of Representatives, Committee on Banking, Finance and Urban Affairs, Subcommittee on the City. *Local Distress, State Surpluses, Proposition 13: Prelude to Fiscal Crisis or New Opportunities?* Hearings held July 25 and 26, 1978. Washington, D.C.: U.S. Government Printing Office, 1978.

U.S. Senate Committee on Finance, Subcommittee on Social Security. *Social Security Financing Proposals.* Hearings held June and July, 1977. Washington, D.C.: U.S. Government Printing Office, 1977.

VROOM, VICTOR H., and EDWARD L. DECI (eds.). *Management and Motivation.* Middlesex, England: Penguin Books, 1970.

WACHTER, MICHAEL L. "The Changing Responsiveness of Wage Inflation," *Brookings Papers on Economic Activity* 1976(1), pp. 115–167.

WALFISH, BEATRICE. "QWL Project at GM Plant Cited as Key to Labor-Management Accord," *World of Work Report* 2(12):133–193, December 1977.

Wall Street Journal. "Paid Public-Service Leaves Buoy Workers, But Return to Old Jobs Can Be Wrenching," May 6, 1981.

WALTON, RICHARD E. "Quality of Working Life: What Is It?" *Sloan Management Review*, Fall 1973, pp. 11–21.

————. "Establishing and Maintaining High Commitment Work Systems," in John R. Kimberly and Robert H. Miles (eds.), *The Organizational Life Cycle.* San Francisco: Jossey-Bass, 1980; pp. 208–290.

WILLIAMS, ERVIN (ed.). *Participative Management: Concepts, Theory and Implementation.* Atlanta: Georgia State University, 1976.

WILLIAMSON, OLIVER E. *Markets and Hierarchies.* New York: Free Press, 1975.

WINPISINGER, WILLIAM W. "In the Real World, We Have to Eat," *Viewpoint* 8(3); Washington, D.C.: Industrial Union Department, AFL-CIO, 1978.

World of Work Report. Scarsdale, N.Y.: Work in America Institute, monthly.

ZWERDLING, DANIEL. "At IGP, It's Not Business as Usual," *Working Papers for a New Society* 5(1):68–81, Spring 1977.

INDEX